The

Volume 2

Preaching on the Old Testament

'Go and say to this people . . .'

Christine Pilkington

ISBN 1 85852 173 4

In remembrance

of my mother,
Edith Pilkington
(1916-1998)

and of her friend, my teacher,
Dorothy Redmayne
(1913-1999)
who for so many years
loved to preach on the Old Testament

May the wisdom of the Wonderful Counsellor guide you,
the strength of the Mighty God defend you,
the love of the Everlasting Father enfold you,
and the peace of the Prince of Peace be upon you.

Christine Pilkington is Principal Lecturer in Religious Studies at Canterbury Christ Church University College, where she teaches Old Testament and Jewish Studies. She is a member of the Local Preachers' Studies Board of the Methodist Church and a Fellow of the College of Preachers. Her publications include *Teach Yourself Judaism, Understanding Christian Perspectives,* and *Judaism: an approach for GCSE* (Hodder & Stoughton). She has also contributed Old Testament entries to *Guidelines* (Bible Reading Fellowship) and *Disciple* (Methodist Publishing House).

ABOUT THE SERIES/ INTRODUCTION

Preaching is a very particular form of communication which has always been important in the life of the Christian church. At the beginning of the twenty-first century we are undergoing a revolution in the varieties, method and speed of our communications. Preachers of all denominations, ordained and lay, undertake this calling with an awareness that we preach in a changing context.

The Preacher's Library is designed to help us to think through, perhaps in some cases reassess, why we preach, how we preach, and to whom we preach. Some of the volumes in this series will take a fresh look at familiar issues, such as how preachers should approach various parts of the Bible, how we understand and express our doctrinal inheritance and the variety of styles in which preaching can be done. Other volumes will introduce issues which may be less familiar to many of us, such as the significance of our cultural context or the way in which the self-understanding of a woman preacher has important things to say to all preachers. Some of these books will offer direct help in the practice of preaching. Others will deal with issues which, although they appear more theoretical, impinge upon the preacher's task and on which we therefore need to have reflected if we are to preach with integrity in today's world.

All the writers in this series, lay and ordained, women and men, are recognised preachers within their own denominations and write with the needs of their colleagues firmly in mind. These books will avoid academic jargon, but they will not avoid dealing with difficult issues. They are offered to other preachers in the belief that as we deepen our thinking and hone our skills God's people will be blessed and built up to the glory of God.

In *Preaching on the Old Testament*, God's command to the prophet, 'Go and say to this people . . .' (Isaiah 6:9) summarises Dr Pilkington's conviction that the Christian preacher must respond to the Old Testament text in this way. It is therefore fittingly used as a sub-title for the book. The author challenges the sometimes unthinking assumption which preachers make that the Old Testament, being obscure, difficult and irrelevant, is better left alone except for a few well-loved passages. She argues that, on the contrary, our congregations need to hear Old Testament based sermons in order to have a fully rounded picture of the God we worship and, indeed, in order to understand much of the New Testament. She explores various kinds of writing to be found within the Old Testament, and offers pointers to how they may be used fruitfully in our preaching. This is a book to challenge and stretch the preacher, but also to kindle enthusiasm for preaching on this significant part of the Christian scriptures.

Michael J Townsend

CONTENTS

INTRODUCTION

The scriptures of the Christian church consist of two parts, an Old and a New Testament. For the first two centuries of its existence, however, the early church had only the Jewish scriptures, as read in the synagogue, articulating and governing its faith. Later it joined them to its own traditions, both written and oral. The very fact that the church laid claim to these scriptures, later to be known as the Old Testament, lays on those within today's church an obligation. But what is the nature of the obligation? The early church claimed that the Jewish scriptures were, in some way, a vital witness to Jesus as the Christ of the New Testament.

This presents us with both an opportunity and a challenge. The lines are usually drawn here between the views of inspiration and authority which emerge from different Christian traditions. It is not the purpose of this book to defend a particular approach. Not all approaches are compatible with each other and discussion will go on. But it is this book's purpose to demonstrate that the Old Testament is part of the church's scriptures. It became so and has stayed so – to this day. Therefore the Christian preacher cannot but be concerned with it.

It is significant that the church never worked out the precise nature of the relationship between Old and New Testaments. It simply affirmed that together they constituted the books judged to be normative for Christianity. Over the centuries there were struggles over issues such as prophecy and fulfilment, law and gospel and these have never been resolved in any specific credal statement. The aim was to do justice to both God and Jesus. Where conflict was perceived, one reaction was to take an Old Testament passage or figure as an allegory or a type of a New Testament passage or figure. Such allegorical and typological interpretations reflect a tension between acknowledging that the New Testament has been influenced by the Old and interpreting the Old Testament on its own terms.

The sub-title of this book takes words addressed to a prophet living in the tiny country of Judah in the eighth century BC. He is commissioned to: 'Go and say to this people . . .' (Isaiah 6:9). 'This people', as the descendants of Isaiah and his people, still exists as the Jewish people. Jews read their scriptures, referred to as the Hebrew Bible or Tenakh, and interpret them as being addressed to them. No reference to the coming of Jesus as the Messiah (the Christ) is necessary, possible, or in any way even desirable in the Jewish interpretation.

Christians, however, cannot read these scriptures as if Jesus had never been. How then are they to become 'this people' addressed by God in the book of Isaiah or any other Old Testament book? Some solve this problem by ensuring that the Old Testament is seldom read in their church services, let alone preached on. There is then no need for any living, breathing Christian to wonder why his or her community should listen to the Old Testament, often perceived as totally remote in time and culture.

Assuming that this is no solution, the question, for the church and its members, remains one of how to do justice to the unique witness of the Old Testament, whilst acknowledging that, in their worship, the Old Testament is always part rather than the whole of the Christian scriptures. How should we interpret what for Jesus was not some sort of background to a new revelation but his entire Bible? Can the church claim continuity as the people of God in its response to the Old Testament and, if so, how?

It is not being argued, of course, that the Old Testament can be interpreted only in the church. The so-called 'academy' of school, college, or university has long been engaged in its critical interpretation, that is, interpretation which takes account of scientific, linguistic and historical developments. This need be no threat to the church's interpretation. A confessional position is assumed in this book in that it is written by a Christian preacher for Christian preachers. This is not seen, by the writer at least, as a severing from the world in which she spends far more time than in the pulpit, namely the academic world and one in which she has a particular interest in the Jewish religion at that. Rather, the hope is that any abilities and insights gained from the latter may feed into the former world.

The Christian preacher wants the congregation to hear 'the living voice of God'. Whatever interpretation he or she has of this phrase, the church should be a place where this might be heard through the reading and exposition of scripture. The reasons why the Old Testament is, nonetheless, often neglected in Christian preaching are all too often heard. Not heard often enough, however, are the reasons why this is greatly to each Christian's loss. Put slightly more positively, the request is: 'Give me one good reason why I should preach on the Old Testament!' In what follows, I hope to give more than one.

From the Old Testament we can take inspiration. Its profundity, breadth, and literary beauty give our message both its source and content. They inspire us to be messengers, heralds, prophets, evangelists, ensuring that our preaching variously encourages, challenges, revives, warns and confirms us in our faith.

In the Old Testament we can find meaning. Drawing on Old Testament scholarship, we can learn and develop skills of exegesis which are sometimes similar to, and at other times different from, those required for New Testament exegesis. The huge variety of content, style and purpose represented in the Old Testament books makes us think creatively about how we get from text to sermon.

From the Old Testament we can preach the gospel. It reminds us that the 'good news' of God's saving love did not suddenly originate in the first century AD. It gives us the root and the content of this claim about God and human beings in ways that may be judged surprising, shocking, and, some would say, incredible. The Old Testament enables us to get a hearing. It has the sense of something worth saying. It contains strong words, gripping stories, and itself provides models of how to communicate powerfully.

The Old Testament encourages us to begin with God. It presents a picture of this God far bigger than we could have from the New Testament alone. Though not a systematic theology, it is essentially theological in its outlook and it provides models and resources for worship and spirituality. The Old Testament commands us to be the people of God. It makes us examine the link between belief and action. It reminds us that the main purpose of preaching is to transform behaviour.

The Old Testament urges us to tell the truth. It directs us to serious claims about God, the world, and interaction between the two. It makes us face the difficult questions which people ask. The Old Testament challenges us to make sense of experience. Its cultural and social diversity suggests that 'all human life is there'. We encounter a wide range of attempts to come to terms with the realities, even the nonsenses, of life against which we can test our own.

If all, or even any, of these arguments prove to have any validity, the preacher is obliged to: 'Go and say to this people . . .'.

1

TAKING INSPIRATION

Unless the preacher is fired up by the Old Testament then it is highly unlikely that the recipients of the sermon will be. If it is accepted that the Old Testament itself can inspire and deepen our faith, then it is incumbent on the preacher to do his or her best to communicate something of this. How to get started, how to take our own inspiration as preachers from the Old Testament, is then a vital matter.

The question essentially concerns exegesis. Some might immediately give up the quest at this point. If exegesis is taken to be the elucidation of a passage verse by verse, or of one verse word by word, they might retort that this is not their style of preaching or even that they think the usefulness of this style of preaching is long dead.

The style and construction of a sermon may or may not be exegetical in the sense just defined. Whatever one's homiletical tastes and preferences, however, there can surely be no Christian preaching which does not in some way at least have its starting-point in the Bible and this Bible includes the Old Testament. I take the starting-point to be long before the final form of the sermon descends on the congregation. It is precisely where the preacher starts, that is, his or her method of sermon preparation. Admittedly, the trigger for some dominant thought or theme might well be not a biblical passage but an event or experience. But I for one do not attend worship wanting to hear about a local, national or international occurrence, however significant. Nor do I go to hear about an experience in the life of the preacher. If I wanted to do this, I could think of far more congenial settings than a church and with far more appropriate accompaniments than hymns and prayers. It is a pity that it is difficult to say this without sounding rather pious, but the fact remains that I go to church to worship God and somehow to link my life, as a member of a worshipping community, with this God who is worthy of worship.

Even if my world is falling in at the time – perhaps supremely then – I do not need the sermon to depict other human miseries or give me a heap of statistics on world poverty or rising divorce rates. These facts may, indeed, be a part of the sermon – if really necessary – but what I need is help in living the life of faith in my present circumstances. Plenty of other sources may be used to construct a sermon which attempts to do this, but if the Bible is not chief among them I think I deserve a refund. Experience is sometimes considered to make what the preacher says, in the much overused word, 'relevant'. In an act of worship it is ignorance of the Bible that can make the preacher irrelevant. I know about my own life and probably a little about the preacher's. What I now want to know is what can be said about it from the perspective of the God I had hoped to hear from.

The preacher is often recommended to sum up the main aim of the sermon in terms of the main content to be communicated, and the main purpose of the communication. The purpose of this sermon is to convey *abc* in order to do *xyz*. (For instance, to explore what Hosea says, in 11:1-11, about God's yearning to forgive his people in order to understand the costliness of forgiveness.) There may not always be three points or three purposes, of course, but there should always be at least one of each. Otherwise, why bother? He or she should do this spelling out of the precise aim throughout the preparation, during the writing (whether this is fully scripted or not), and shortly before the actual delivery. This way he or she pays the listeners the deserved compliment of recognising that they have not come out of vague interest but out of need. That need is communication of belief in such a way as will inspire action.

And the belief is not any old belief, picked up from any old source, but the belief of the Christian whose scripture is the Bible. Accepting, then, that the basic ingredient of the sermon is to be found in the Bible itself, we still need practical ways of first accessing, and then incorporating, this ingredient to best effect.

A most powerful image of a preacher is to be found in Isaiah 50:4, 'The Lord GOD has given me the tongue of a teacher, that I may know how to sustain the weary with a word. Morning by morning he wakens – wakens my ear to listen as those who are taught.' The figure so described has nothing to say until he has listened to God. In this passage (verses 4-9), usually taken to be the words of God's servant, God is the subject of the key verbs in verses 4, 5, 7 and 9. The concentration is not on the servant's work but on God. Only by regular and attentive listening can the servant do his job which, in this case, is primarily to speak. And 'the sustaining word to the weary is not just any pastoral word. It is a word energising the exiles to their own distinctive identity in a context where that identity is at risk.'[1]

In order to unpack this Old Testament image of the preacher, exegesis has been carried out. The whole passage has been read, attention has been directed to the way in which 'the Lord GOD' is mentioned twice as initiating the action. Particularly striking phrases such as 'to sustain the weary with a word' and 'morning by morning' have been paraphrased to draw out their force. And a commentary (in this case from the series *Westminster Bible Companion*) has been used to identify the recipients of the preacher's message and their historical circumstances which make them in such need of a word which gives them reassurance that they are God's people with a particular task.

This last statement goes beyond what is in the immediate passage before us and draws on the whole of Isaiah 40-55. The expositor may have come to conclusions about the Babylonian exile simply from reading Isaiah 40-55 or he or she may have consulted one or more commentaries on these chapters. The type of commentary, especially in terms of details and of whether it refers to the original

Hebrew, can be chosen by the exegete according to his or her requirements. Even without a knowledge of Hebrew, the exegete might have become interested in, for instance, the footnote to verse 4 in the New Revised Standard Version. It explains that the Hebrew speaks right away of 'those who are taught', as do the closing words of verse 4. Why, then, has the NRSV departed from the rendering as we find it in the Revised Standard Version which renders the Hebrew identically in both occurrences? This may fascinate you and you may get an answer from a commentary. This sort of enquiry may not interest you at all and it may be hard to see what difference it would make to your preaching.

The last point aside, however, what has just happened to Isaiah 50:4-9 is a clear example of the benefits of exegesis. Without exegesis, the passage might be ignored, or it might be seized upon as the third of four passages often singled out from the book of Isaiah as the 'suffering servant songs' (42:1-4; 49:1-6; 52:13-53:12). The temptation of the Christian preacher might be simply then to leap straight to the New Testament, identify the servant with Jesus, and proceed not to pay close attention to what is said about the servant (strangely enough not called such in verses 4-9 whilst verse 10 does explicitly mention God's servant – which raises a question in itself for those so inclined) thus giving the Old Testament merely a nod and a wink. The only question being asked becomes: 'Who is the servant?' and the answer is prematurely and rather inconsequentially given as Christ. No harm done, you may say. Within a Christian service, probably not. But why should we be so negative? We are surely aiming to do more than avoid harm. We are aiming to draw on all our biblical resources to do good. Our quest here, as throughout this volume, is for how the Old Testament may enrich our preaching.

This Isaiah passage occurs as the Old Testament lesson for the Principal Service on the Second Sunday of the Passion in all three years of the cycle in the Revised Common Lectionary. In each case, the Psalm is 31:9-16 (an appeal from God's 'servant', verse 16, to rescue him from suffering) and the Epistle is Philippians 2:5-11 (an early Christian hymn to Christ whom God exalted because of his obedience 'to the point of death', verse 8). There is a choice of gospel, in Year A from Matthew, in Year B from Mark, and in Year C from Luke, but all six possible gospel passages are from the Passion Narrative.

It may be added that the lectionary compilers judge there to be a division before verse 9b which they take with the verse which follows and so offer the passage as Isaiah 50:4-9a. Again, there will be some but by no means all who feel obliged to investigate the whys and wherefores of the division at this point, though doing so may well contribute to the interpretation of the passage. Certainly, it is no academic exercise, especially when the preacher is not the person who is going to read the passage publicly. Precisely where a passage begins and ends can have consequences for the effectiveness of the impressive Old Testament sermon about to be delivered. (See further chapter 4.)

Now there is nothing, of course, to stop the preacher from tackling Isaiah 50:4-9a/b on a different Sunday in the Christian year. However, the fact that it features on Palm Sunday in itself contributes to the passage's interpretation. This ecumenical lectionary, particularly in what it refers to as 'Ordinary time', encourages us not to try to spot some theme which unites the week's lectionary passages. In many cases no such theme exists. The thought is that a pressing of all biblical material into themes may straight-jacket the material and not 'let the Bible speak for itself' as we may curiously put it. Nonetheless, in Special time, that is, seasonal times of the year, such as Advent or Lent, the appropriate Christian festival will intentionally inform the interpretation of the Old Testament passage. Thus it would be very curious if the suffering of the servant as a direct result of his ministry (50:6-9) were not to loom large in the exposition of this particular passage in Passiontide.

Nevertheless, one of the great advantages of the preacher's turning to the commentaries early in his or her preparation is that important aspects of the passage are allowed to stimulate the mind in ways in which the New Testament passages alone and their focus on Jesus could not do. The sheer faithfulness of the speaker, for instance, both in tapping into God so that his strength is 'new every morning' and in relying on this strength against all odds, has something important to say both to the preacher and to every member of the congregation, whatever his or her particular 'ministry' and 'suffering'.

This passage from Isaiah has been chosen for this extended focus partly because of the model it offers of the preacher but also because, together with the other three passages traditionally linked together as 'suffering servant songs', it illustrates very well some of the possibilities and pitfalls of following the Old Testament lectionary readings. What has been described as 'the crescendo of suffering' in these four servant passages has a particular force in Passiontide when the Christian focus is on the way in which suffering is not incidental but fundamental to the nature of the servant's task. But we need the exegesis on Isaiah 50:4-9, preferably with at least the preacher's understanding of this strand of suffering in the other three 'servant songs', without initial reference to Jesus as servant shutting down all further interest.

Another strength of the Revised Common Lectionary is that, outside Seasonal time, the biblical books are read semi-continuously. This affords a real chance, first for the preacher and then for the congregation, to concentrate on one biblical book. If one of the factors putting off a preacher from preaching on the Old Testament is that he or she feels daunted by the sheer size of the enterprise, trying to get acquainted with the very varied historical settings, forms and messages of the various Old Testament books, then concentrating on just one may be a golden opportunity. This requires forward planning and much church co-operation, especially where a preacher does not occupy the same pulpit from week to week. We should also remember that the congregation has not come to hear a course of lectures on the Old Testament, nor should people who are not present every week feel disadvantaged if a series on one book is conducted.

If the one book approach is followed, then the erstwhile avoider of the Old Testament might feel inclined to purchase a couple of volumes to help give the feeling of really getting to grips with something. Two series are particularly helpful here. The first is the Old Testament Guides (there is also a New Testament series), published by JSOT Press, an imprint of Sheffield Academic Press. With the exception of Robert Carroll's volume on Jeremiah, which, though very useful, for some reason seems to assume a more advanced knowledge, this series offers an excellent introduction to each Old Testament book. The overview is clear, comforting, up-to-date, stimulating – and short. Each is written by a scholar with a particular enthusiasm for his or her chosen book. There is, in the series, one volume on every single Old Testament book, though sometimes shorter books have been combined, eg Rex Mason's volumes on Micah, Nahum, Obadiah (1991) and Zephaniah, Habakkuk, Joel (1994). (Details of many other volumes in this series will be given in 'Further Reading' at the end of the following chapters of this book.)

The journal *Worship & Preaching*, itself a source of help with its regular 'preaching notes' which include brief exegesis, carried in 1977-1978 a series of articles reviewing most commentaries then available on the major biblical books. Another series featured between 1992-1994. Michael Townsend, the author of the articles, adopted the particular criterion of 'usefulness to preachers'. To quote from his introductory article:

> In general terms, it is taken to mean that a commentary which devotes almost all its space to discussing linguistic and/or historical critical matters is likely to be less helpful than a commentary which, whilst not neglecting these, does something to help the reader understand the possible meanings the text might have for today. At the other extreme a commentary which jumps straight from the Bible into today's world, spoonfeeds us in ways which are not helpful either. No commentary, however user-friendly, exempts us from the need to wrestle with the text. A good commentary, for the preacher, is one which helps to bring a biblical passage alive for us,

> suggests ways of understanding it which we can use in preaching, and alerts us to any pitfalls in interpretation of which we might otherwise have been unaware.[2]

This is not the place to give a summary of the verdicts there given on each Old Testament commentary against this criterion. To be mentioned as often coming out of the survey quite well is the Daily Study Bible series, published by Saint Andrew Press (for example, K T Aitkin's *Proverbs*, 1986, Robert Davidson's *Jeremiah and Lamentations*, 1983/5 and G A F Knight's *Leviticus*, 1981). Also recommended is the series of Epworth Commentaries, for example, C S Rodd's *Job*, 1990. This series, based on the Revised English Bible, is described by its publishers, Epworth Press, as 'written by experienced scholars for the use of ministers, preachers, teachers, students and church leaders' specifically to 'relate the texts in their ancient settings to the needs of Christians in a multi-racial, multi-faith society'. Already published are Stacey's *Isaiah 1-39*, Mowvley's *Amos and Hosea*, McKeating's *Jeremiah*, Biggs' *Ezekiel* and Coggins' *Exodus*. Forthcoming are: Clements' *Deuteronomy*, Curtis' *Psalms*, and Thompson's *Isaiah 40-66*.

Methodist preachers in training are given a certain amount of Old Testament in the *Faith & Worship* course. For example, portions of Amos and Isaiah are studied in Unit 15 – 'The Prophets'. Perhaps one of the above mentioned Guides and/or Epworth Commentaries could feature regularly in everyone's Continuous Local Preacher Development or equivalent. Whether or not the lectionary is always followed in worship – and it is recognised that there may be good reasons for its not being – its existence is itself a help to preachers wanting to preach on the Old Testament. Further encouragement comes, of course, from the Revised Common Lectionary's provision of a psalm for every single service, that is, for the 'Principal Service' which sometimes has a choice of two lections (one 'continuous' and one 'related' in which there is a clear thematic link between all the readings for that day) and the one lection for the 'Second Service'. This reflects the emphasis of the Roman Catholic Church, in which this lectionary originated, on the corporate hearing of scripture in Christian worship. It might, of course, be judged enough, or even better, just to read or sing a psalm and not to preach on it. Certainly one could do much worse, especially if it is followed by silence or some sort of meditation. The unique value of the psalms for expressing both the individual's and the community's faith will, however, be considered further since, in itself, this constitutes a major reason for preaching on the Old Testament.

Another promising series is *A Biblical Exegesis for Sunday's Sermon*, edited by Roger Van Harn, (Wm B Eerdmans Publishing Company). Each of its three volumes (the first containing Old Testament lections in 2001) is based on one year of the three-year cycle of the Revised Common Lectionary. Every 1500 word chapter addresses the question: 'What does the preacher need to know about this lesson in order to preach a faithful sermon from it?' The response comprises the story of 'what God said and did in the history of Israel and in the person of Jesus Christ for the salvation of the world', 'explanation of the text's features that may obscure meanings because of differences in language and culture', and illumination from the exegesis of the text of 'features of current culture or characteristics of the church that call for celebration or judgement'.

2

FINDING MEANING

In preparing a sermon, the preacher has the task of interpreting the biblical text (used in the sense of a passage/reading/lection rather than necessarily one or two verses). Exegesis is a fundamental part of this, but not the whole of it. For the preacher has to address a specific audience on a 'concrete' occasion in a way that goes beyond what might happen in a study or classroom. The results of the preparatory exegesis are a means to this public end. To harness the strengths of exegesis, however, the preacher has to decide what rules apply.

The overall search is for meaning. A differentiation is sometimes made between the so-called 'original' meaning of a text and the meaning which it later acquires. The first can be arrived at by what is sometimes called 'traditio-historical criticism', establishing the time and place of the original speaker/reader/hearer of the words. The second depends on times and places which are new in the sense of not being known to the first speaker/reader/hearer. In both cases, the task is exegetical, in the sense of drawing out the meaning of the text. Some prefer to limit the term 'exegesis' to the first quest or to what might be called 'first order questions', such as in the exegesis triangle of the grid towards the end of this chapter. This grid then puts questions about meaning 'acquired' later, as distinct from original, in the other triangles headed 'Preacher/People/Worship'. (It probably does not matter precisely how these questions are referred to, as long as they get asked of each scripture passage.)

In recent years, however, it has come to be realised that establishing the 'original' meaning of a biblical text may simply be impossible. This is not meant to be discouraging of exegetical method, but rather to widen it up. There is as a result an array of disciplines, all of which may be described as biblical exegesis. Even in the world of teaching as distinct from preaching, traditio-historical methods have been judged to have their limitations. These methods comprise what are variously called grammatical criticism, literary criticism, tradition criticism, source criticism, and redaction criticism. More recent methods include narrative criticism, structuralist criticism, canonical criticism, feminist criticism and reader-response criticism.[1] They all, in their different ways, stress the way in which the written text is not, and perhaps never was, static. The reader, whether within biblical times, or in the later history of a community, or today's community, is always playing a part in the interpretation.

Even within the Old Testament itself, it would seem that a process is at work in expounding God's message to people of one time in terms which apply to people of another time. As long ago as 1970, E W Nicholson demonstrated, at least to many people's satisfaction, that the prose material in the book of Jeremiah (as distinct from the prophetic oracles which took the form of poetry) could be described as 'preaching'.[2] Thus what appears to be a narrative about the faithless King Jehoiakim (late seventh century BC) dramatically disposing of a collection of Jeremiah's messages of doom (36:1-27) is, in the form in which it appears in the Bible, an address to the Babylonian exiles (well into the next century), warning them not to reject the prophetic message and to be attentive to the fact that it cannot be destroyed, as clinched in the final part of the chapter where Jeremiah's message is written out all over again (36:27-32). Nor, says Nicholson, is judgement the last word, as a later collection is made of messages of hope. (Though this is recorded in the earlier chapter 30:2, it is undisputed that the chapters of the book of Jeremiah are not arranged chronologically.) And, by the time any of these messages are being read, the editor of the book has a theological framework which includes the message that God's judgement is not an end in itself but a means to restoration. The editor and those for whom he edits Jeremiah's words are not interested in simple recall or reminiscence but in what these words mean for them.

Even at this early juncture, some people's hackles may rise. Are you telling me that the man Jeremiah did not actually say, word for word, what he is recorded as saying? The worry is then of a dangerous slope down which the entire Old Testament slips into inauthenticity. (Needless to say, Christians who feel like this become even more anxious when any similar method of interpretation is applied to the New Testament, especially to the gospels.) A spirited defence may follow of the eternal relevance of God's word to his people. 'The Bible says . . .', begins each statement as if we somehow see words on a page and derive meaning from them which is ancient and automatic, in some way by-passing all that makes up each person's capacity to understand words.

Unfortunately, this apparently protective stance threatens to destroy the very communication to which the Bible testifies. Whether in respect of the Old Testament or the New, each reader/listener has to do some interpretative work before the Bible says anything at all. Take even some of the most popular Old Testament texts and apply to them the 'skip the interpretation' approach. The Bible says: 'The Lord is my shepherd.' What? Now, do not interpret this in any way. 'The Lord is my shepherd' and that is it. Staying with Psalm 23, 'Surely goodness and mercy shall follow me all the days of my life.' What? And 'I shall dwell in the house of the LORD my whole life long.' What? I defy anyone to shut down all his or her mental faculties and then find any meaning in these phrases which have carried such power for people even in their darkest time. (If it be objected that interpretation is required with this psalm because it involves poetic imagery, a similar test of meaning may be tried against a more 'straightforward' narrative, for example, Ezra 3:10-11. What, for instance, does it mean to say that 'God is good'?)

The previous chapter stressed scripture as the starting-point for the preacher's preparation, suggesting that at least one commentary ought to be consulted. What it did not assume was that the preacher's initial inspiration might be some topic, theme or event, after which he or she then turned to scripture, either to a passage which sprang to mind, especially if this is the tradition of the church concerned or, if wanting the discipline and assistance of a set passage, to the lectionary. Reading the biblical passage is obviously vital. At what point the commentary is consulted is perhaps a matter of what works best for the individual. Some people find that a commentary gives not only initial stimulus but also the security of knowing that they are somehow in touch with the people of God over the ages. They may also be nervous that if they do not start with the commentary they might not only misinterpret the biblical text but not interpret it at all, that is, not find that it makes much sense to them. Others prefer to read the lectionary and then keep off the commentary whilst they get on with the everyday life of the week, mulling over the passage. Yet others do not have one standard method, but vary the procedure according to what they find happens when they first read the passage. Not engaging with a biblical passage at all is, as suggested in the previous chapter, not an option for Christian preaching. The resultant sermon may be an airing of views but what connects these with the scripture which the congregation at least expects to be put in touch with?

The proliferation of contemporary methods of interpretation offers an opportunity to the preacher. It is here assumed that there is a vital place for discussing Old Testament texts from the point of view of the traditional historical critical methods. Yet, it is recognised that the emphasis on understanding the text's origins and purpose entirely within its historical setting can obscure ways of relating the Old Testament to contemporary needs and issues. Not all the more recent approaches will appeal to every preacher. Nor can each be applied equally to the many different genres of Old Testament material. Indeed, any preacher who tried the full range would be confused and confusing, not to mention a little exhausted. The line taken in this book is not to make a strict division between traditional and 'modern' methods as if they were rivals, but rather to draw on a variety, seeing how they might complement each other.

In this and the next chapter particularly (and at various points in the chapters which follow), some of the possibilities of this raft of exegetical methods will be indicated. Nonetheless, as in most books about preaching and in most courses for preachers, the merits of historical criticism will be heavily relied on, whilst recognising some of its limitations. Some of the benefits of the traditional approach for the preacher are that, over against an emphasis on our questioning the Old Testament world, it directs us to the Old Testament itself, giving a starting-point in a collection of books not of our choosing. The nature of this collection and its contents challenge us to think in different ways.

Over against our own perspectives and biases, it demands that we do not assume the Old Testament writers had the same agenda as ours. It warns us against overrating our own experiences as the central message of our preaching. In contrast to the fluidity and variety of contemporary experience, it assumes a historical continuity, not in the sense that we can ever get back to Jacob at Bethel (Genesis 28), for instance, but in the sense that we assume that some of the significance of what has been transmitted to us corresponds to what happened to him there.

Over against an emphasis on how the text functions today, it reminds us of the range of forms represented in the Old Testament. This might stop us from trying to press any one of them into a mode which is inappropriate and which distorts its meaning. We recognise in everyday speech, for example, that certain modes are to be interpreted in particular ways. We do not expect imagery in love poetry, 'My love is like a red, red rose', for example, to be taken literally, and we do not expect a riddle to be solved by reference to logic or the dictionary. Traditional form-criticism has given us vital insights into the different purposes of different Old Testament genres.

Some particularly helpful contributions from the contemporary methods will now be outlined. Before, or alongside, the question: 'What echoes are there in this Bible passage for me?', a useful question might be: 'What echoes are there in this Bible passage for the writer/transmitter of the Bible passage?' It is recognised, for instance, that there are what have been called intertextual links between passages in Jeremiah and Hosea, Jeremiah and Ezekiel, and, in a rather different way, between Jeremiah and the Psalms, and between Isaiah 40-55 and the Psalms. The 'writers' of each of these books have all been 'readers' of other texts. Resonances of meaning are not something invented in the last few decades, but something common to the interpretation of texts over the millennia. Questions in the 'Worship' triangle in the grid draw particularly on this intertextuality.

Reader-response is not so much one method but a range of methods, all of which stress the ideas and thoughts coming from a reader engaging with the text. A number of the questions on the grid relate to this approach, especially those in the 'Preacher' triangle. The text itself does not entirely or even mainly direct the act of reading. Rather the reader, or, even more in the church context, a community of readers, contributes to the meaning of the text.

Not being tied to the single agenda of 'What did the text mean?' can free the preacher up to find fascinating, surprising, and compelling interpretations of the text. Instead of the forced attempts to modernise (eg 'Aren't we all really like Jacob in our business dealings?'), this approach may help us truly to engage with contemporary questions. We may be obliged to ask, in relation to the moral ambiguities involved in stories about Abraham, Sarah and Isaac, for instance, 'What does God want?'[3]

Narrative criticism emphasises understanding the Bible as story. This involves readers in a process of engagement, drawing them into the world of the text. It connects the reader to the stories through imaginative identification and focuses attention on issues of plot, character and relationship. (See especially chapter 7.) Through this process, the congregation can begin to see itself as the most recent in a series of communities all telling their particular stories about God's relationship to the world. Sometimes such accounts can be held up as mirrors, showing how horrific stories about a particular group in the ancient world draw into the same field of vision horrors visited on the same group today. This is the technique used, for example, by the literary critic Phyllis Trible, who takes Hagar, whose story is told in Genesis, as symbolic of today's oppressed:

> She is the faithful maid exploited, the black woman used by the male and abused by the female of the ruling class, the surrogate mother, the resident alien without legal recourse, the other woman, the runaway youth, the religious fleeing from affliction, the pregnant young woman alone, the expelled wife, the divorced mother with child, the shopping bag lady carrying bread and water, the homeless woman, the indigent relying upon handouts from the power structures, the welfare mother, and the self-effacing female whose own identity shrinks in service of others.[4]

It has to be admitted, however, that some modern methods are inaccessible to any preacher not following higher degree studies in them – perhaps even then. Even both books mentioned in the notes as examples of approaches especially useful to the preacher (that is, Trible's and Gunn and Fewell's) are not an easy read. Commentaries which attempt to link the preacher with the fruits of many different approaches in relation to particular Old Testament passages, such as the Epworth Series mentioned in the previous chapter, are much to be welcomed.

In everyday life, the messiness of communication, whether written or oral, as it occurs between two people or groups of people is obvious. This is not so much a matter of actual misunderstanding, but of communication always being filtered through personalities. Inevitably, each speaks out of his or her own specific situation and the other person hears also from his or her situation. A great deal of work is being done by the preacher when reading/hearing an Old Testament passage. Even more is being done by the congregation as it hears the preacher's treatment of it. As preachers, we sometimes become dismayed when it becomes evident that someone has heard us say 'something we did not say'. But we all know, again from ordinary conversation, that something we say may take on a different, and not necessarily inferior, significance for someone else. Moreover, we may well have experienced the fascinating way in which something we say gains a meaning, even for ourselves, above that we intended when we uttered the words. The Old Testament itself often speaks of the dynamism of words. As such they cannot be recalled and nor can their effects. This is, indeed, often true to experience.

Below is the blank grid* offered in Unit 2 of the course *Faith & Worship.*[5] Taking any passage from the lectionary, the preacher may then move either from segment to segment filling in the grid, or may complete one segment at a time. Whichever order this is done in, the idea is that the traditional approach via commentary is combined with what might be called new approaches. Below ** are the sort of questions which might help the preacher. Scripture, whether or not the sermon is what might be called expository in terms of resting on a detailed exposition of the passage, is in the centre and all the other four points of reference, including exegesis, are judged essential to constructing a sermon.

The unit then offers an example of a grid completed with Isaiah 40:1-11 as the central Old Testament passage. This includes reference to Mark 1:1-8 which, together with Isaiah 40:1-11, constitutes part of the Revised Common Lectionary for the Principal service on the second Sunday of Advent, Year B. Similarly, the Principal service on the fifth Sunday in 'Ordinary time' combines Isaiah 40:21-31 with Mark 1:29-39. I once heard this passage in Mark preached on in the light of the Isaiah passage. Perhaps this does not count strictly as preaching on the Old Testament, since Mark was the focus. To my mind, it did count, however, since the sort of God depicted in Isaiah 40:21-31 was essential to the exposition of Mark 1:29-39 in terms of how Jesus found a praying-place where he could draw on the resources of his God.

* See page 22 ** See page 23

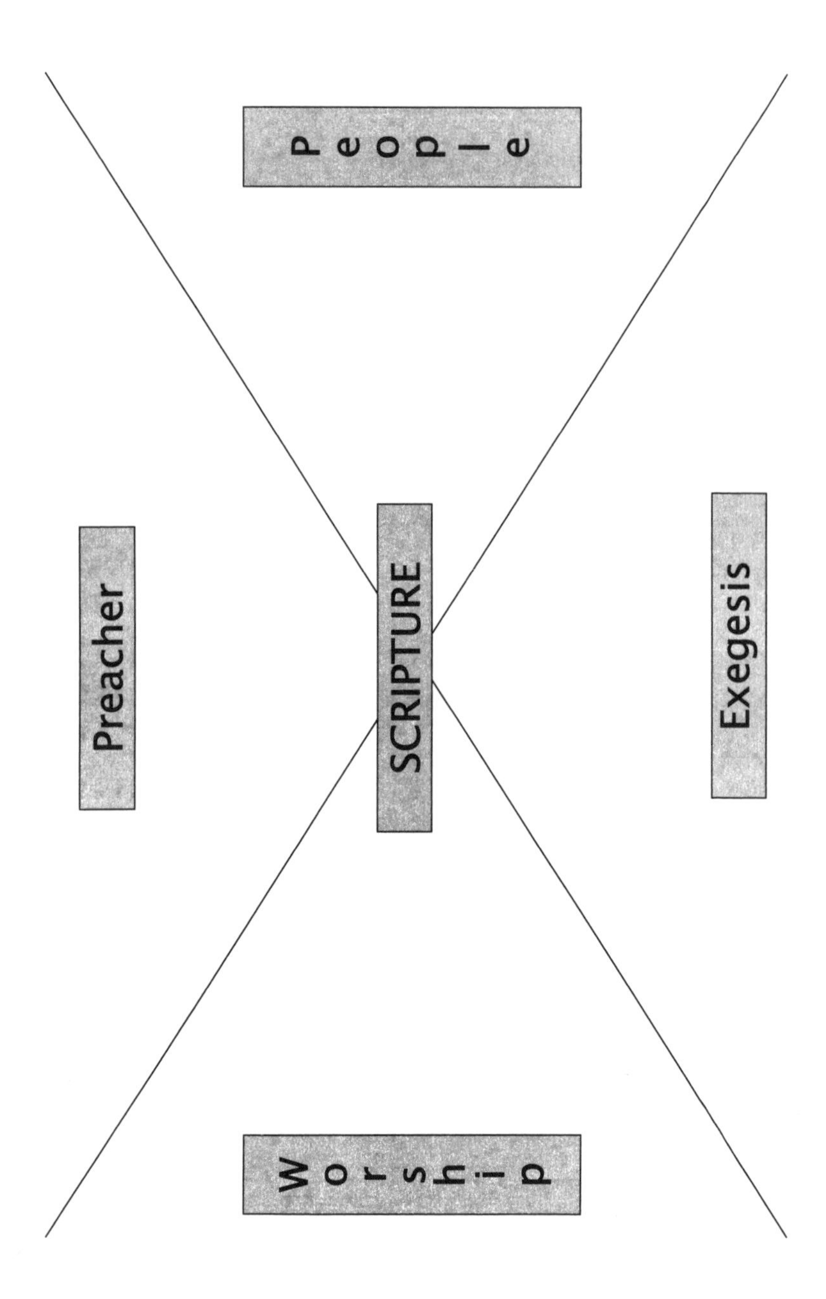
People
Preacher
SCRIPTURE
Exegesis
Worship

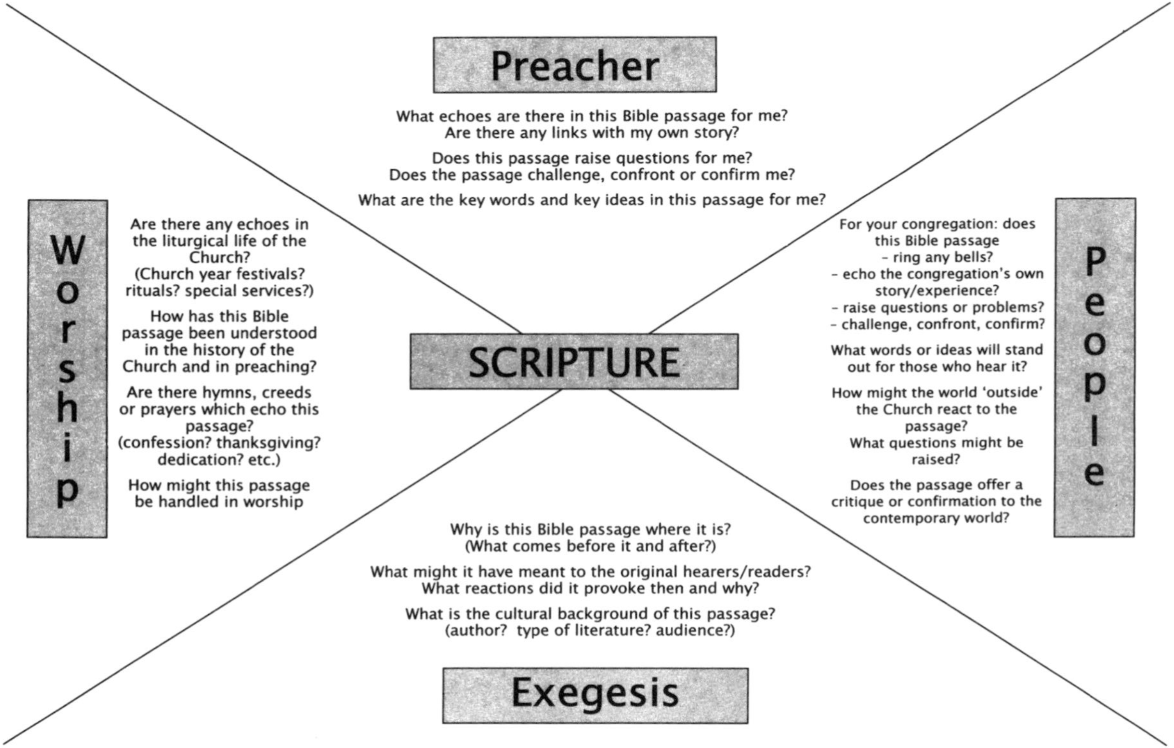

Preacher

What echoes are there in this Bible passage for me?
Are there any links with my own story?

Does this passage raise questions for me?
Does the passage challenge, confront or confirm me?

What are the key words and key ideas in this passage for me?

Worship

Are there any echoes in the liturgical life of the Church?
(Church year festivals? rituals? special services?)

How has this Bible passage been understood in the history of the Church and in preaching?

Are there hymns, creeds or prayers which echo this passage?
(confession? thanksgiving? dedication? etc.)

How might this passage be handled in worship

SCRIPTURE

People

For your congregation: does this Bible passage
- ring any bells?
- echo the congregation's own story/experience?
- raise questions or problems?
- challenge, confront, confirm?

What words or ideas will stand out for those who hear it?

How might the world 'outside' the Church react to the passage?
What questions might be raised?

Does the passage offer a critique or confirmation to the contemporary world?

Exegesis

Why is this Bible passage where it is?
(What comes before it and after?)

What might it have meant to the original hearers/readers?
What reactions did it provoke then and why?

What is the cultural background of this passage?
(author? type of literature? audience?)

The first part of the 'sermon' was, in fact, done by asking each member of the congregation to discuss with the neighbouring person what struck them about the picture of God in the Old Testament passage. This discussion was fed back in not by asking for the results of the discussion – often quite difficult acoustically in a church building – but by the preacher's developing, in the sermon proper, some of the conclusions which he imagined might have arisen for most pairs. The experience reminded me that preaching need not always take the form of a traditional one person sermon. Indeed, it could be argued that preaching may sometimes not involve a sermon as such at all. Some might feel short-changed by this, but I wonder if it might not be worth trying out the grid and its questions in relation to any chosen Old Testament lectionary reading and then the preacher considering whether one, or any combination of music, silence, non-biblical reading, drama, mime or other activity which helps promote the thoughts which he or she puts into the grid, might constitute the preaching on the Old Testament. The preparation is no less, but the method of delivery may be creative and stimulating for preacher and congregation alike.

Further Reading

John Barton, *People of the Book?* SPCK, London 1988.
Fred B Craddock, *Preaching*, Abingdon Press, Nashville 1985.
John Goldingay, *Models for Interpretation of Scripture*, Eerdmans Publishing Co., Grand Rapids 1995. (This is a more detailed and technical work.)

3

PREACHING THE GOSPEL

Whatever the scripture passage being preached on, the task of the Christian preacher is indisputably to preach the gospel or good news. This good news is not any old announcement, but one specifically linked to the ministry of Jesus. The aim is for the preacher's life and the lives of the members of the congregation to be affected by this gospel. Thus the collect for the service of Admission of Local Preachers in *The Methodist Worship Book* reads:

> Lord our God,
> as we rejoice in the ministry of preaching,
> let the Gospel of your Son come to us,
> not in words alone, but in power and love;
> that through our life and witness
> the world may believe.[1]

But the Old Testament does not mention Jesus, so the question remains: 'What is the Christian preacher doing preaching on the Old Testament?' Put starkly, it could be worded: 'What makes Christian preaching Christian?' Will the fact that an Old Testament sermon occurs in Christian worship automatically make it a proclamation of the gospel? Is it the framework of Christian hymns and prayers which alters it from being a Jewish sermon on the Hebrew Bible? Certainly, there will always be the crucial difference in Christian worship that a reading from the New Testament will also feature, but in what way will its gospel relate to the Old Testament passage and a sermon thereon? The congregation is hardly to be blamed for a tendency always to come at the Old Testament through New Testament eyes, for the very fact that there is without fail a New Testament lesson encourages that. If the preacher does not altogether want this, or wants something different to be said about the Old Testament, then he or she will first have to work it out, and then spell it out.

The New Testament itself uses the Old Testament in more than one way. Sometimes it simply quotes a text and then claims its fulfilment in Jesus and/or his disciples (eg Hosea 11:1 and Matthew 2:15). At other times, it claims to be drawing out a meaning implicit in an Old Testament text (eg Psalm 110:1 and Mark 12:35-37). These 'proof texts' are designed to demonstrate to the followers of the new religion a continuity with the old. And yet, by its very nature, the new covenant claims a discontinuity with the old covenant at points which, to the satisfaction of Christians at least, explains why a new religion was necessary. Such lifting of Old Testament passages out of their 'original' context and reapplying them can strike the modern reader as forced if not altogether false. But, whatever the precise method of application, what the New Testament is claiming centres on the concept of fulfilment. This concept lies also at the heart of the use of the Old Testament in Christian worship, with readings from both Testaments, interspersed with hymns and prayers which draw variously on words and ideas from both Testaments. The question arises: 'How should the preacher, aware of a range of critical methods of interpretation, handle the whole question of the Old Testament's being fulfilled in the New?'

There are various ways, in Christian preaching, of approaching the matter of fulfilment. One is always to pair an Old Testament text with a New Testament text. This is what Elizabeth Achtemeier has long argued.[2] Wary of turning the Old Testament into a collection of timeless truths, she insists on the essentially historical nature of the faiths of both Testaments. If we take Hosea 1:6-9 and 2:23 without a complementary New Testament text, for example, all we can do with them is get their general gist, namely that God has rejected Israel as his people because of their behaviour and then apply this directly to us, paying little heed to what specifically Hosea was criticising in eighth century Israel. Instead, she argues, we must go on to the claim of the New Testament that, as Christians, we now are God's people (1 Peter 2:10, quoting Hosea). What we are thereby asserting is that the same God who acted in Hosea's times acts in ours and in recognisable ways. The root of Achtemeier's thesis is: 'The Old Testament becomes a part of our Bible, of our canon, only because Christ Jesus is its final interpretation and fulfillment.'[3]

Achtemeier is arguing for the necessity of Old Testament preaching in Christian worship but not everyone will find her line of argument or her method satisfactory. It is not clear, for instance, why inattention to the specific misdemeanours of Hosea's contemporaries is the inevitable consequence of our taking only an Old Testament text, rather than one from each Testament, in Christian worship. Her conviction that God acts as saviour in the history of humankind is one that is accepted in this volume as a key to a faith community as it interprets the Bible. It is a particular emphasis of canonical criticism, resting on more traditional biblical theology. To adopt it as the one and only thing to be said in Old Testament preaching, however, strikes me as dangerous, not just because I feel a certain history-fatigue coming on, but because it threatens to shut down the dynamic of biblical interpretation. It surely rejects not only the many possible gains from the 'new' methods but also some from the 'old' methods too.

Achtemeier's Old Testament interpretation insists on taking Jesus as its starting-point. He and his community of faith are Israel as she is meant to be. This can be seen in the many examples of paired texts, with the headings, which she offers:

Hosea 1:1-9 and Romans 1:18-32
'God's Judgement upon Us'
Hosea 1:1-9 and John 11:45-53
'The Reversal of Judgement'
Hosea 3:1-5 and Luke 5:27-39
'Repentance and Discipline'

Hosea 2:14-15 and Matthew 6:25-33
'Our Love Affair with God'
Hosea 2:16-20 and Philippians 3:12-16 or Revelation 21:1-4
'The Final Vision'
Hosea 4:1-2 and 2 Corinthians 11:2 or Ephesians 5:32
'Our Relation to God as a Marriage'
Hosea 13:4-6 and John 14:1-11
'On Knowing God'
Hosea 5:3-4 and Romans 6:6-11
'Our Slavery to Sin'
Hosea 11:1-11 and Galatians 4:3-7
'Our Adoption as Sons'
Hosea 5:15-6:6 and Matthew 7:21-23
'The Nature of True Worship'
Hosea 9:15 and Romans 8:31-34
'Is God for Us or against Us?'

Achtemeier's model may be helpful as one among many and it certainly shows the potential of the Old Testament book of Hosea for preaching. By taking seriously an exposition of Hosea's message to 'his own time' she also manages to avoid simply turning the Old Testament into a series of predictions – a recurrent danger amongst Christian preachers perhaps wondering what else to do with it. (The way the Old Testament readings are introduced in 'Nine Lessons and Carols', as, for instance, from King's College Chapel on Christmas Eve – 'the prophet foretells . . .' – always makes me nervous in this regard.) There are other methods of relating Old and New Testaments, however, and other ways of coming at the whole issue of fulfilment.

One of these illustrates the way in which so-called 'literary approaches' to biblical interpretation may liberate us to do justice to both Old and New Testaments in Christian preaching. It avoids relentlessly tying us to Jesus as the start of all our thinking. Yet it also avoids distorting the vital and undeniable fact that, for Christians, all that God intended (and surely this is not yet known even in Christianity), is somehow found in Jesus. So this approach speaks more of hopes realised than of predictions fulfilled. In this regard, it resembles Achtemeier's method to some degree. A good example can be found in Isaiah 7:14. Matthew 1:22-23 quotes

Isaiah's words and applies them to Jesus. At this point, Christians often divide. There are those who emphasise the authority of both Matthew and Isaiah as testimony to the virgin birth of Jesus. No matter that the Hebrew word for 'virgin' is not used in Isaiah 7:14 whilst a word meaning specifically 'young woman' is. And there are those who emphasise this point of language and the historical context of Isaiah's words and say that Matthew is pulling an Old Testament text out of context, even misusing it when he chooses the Greek word for 'virgin' to translate the Hebrew. (They may then go further, claiming that 'proof' of the virgin birth is thus weakened.)

But need it be either/or? Are there no approaches to interpretation which enable us to take seriously Isaiah's words of warning to King Ahaz in a specific political crisis whilst taking equally seriously the meaning these words have come to have in Christian usage? This is not to claim Christian usage as the only valid one. When read in the synagogue, today just as much as in Jesus' day, Isaiah 7:14 makes full and perfect sense without any reference to Christianity. But it is to claim Christian usage as Christian, simply because the reader or hearer of the text is Christian. He or she occupies a different world from the Jewish reader or hearer of this text. Consequently, the world of meaning is different. This is not to slip into saying that both traditions are the same or that they are interchangeable to members of either tradition. It is to give a way of claiming the Old Testament as an essential part of the canon of Christian scripture which is different from, and some would say, more dynamic than the Achtemeier model allows for.

It also allows the preacher to discover meaning which has something to say in a way that might affect both belief and behaviour – surely the purpose of preaching. The exegetical questions: 'What might it have meant to the original hearers/readers?' and 'What reactions did it provoke then and why?' can sensibly be answered from the historical context of Isaiah 7:1-17. Against the background of a military threat from Syria and Israel, King Ahaz of Judah is told that a young woman will give birth to a son and that, before he is old enough to choose between good and bad, the threat will have disappeared. The message is typical of that given by this prophet when kings are showing a lack of trust in God who, the prophet believes, is in charge of historical events (eg Isaiah 10:5-11; 30:15-17; 31:1-9). At the very heart of the sign with which God offers to reassure Ahaz is the naming of the son (again a common way of communicating a message – see Isaiah 7:3; 8:1 and Hosea 1). The name 'Immanuel' expresses the reason why Ahaz should not fret, namely that 'God is with us.' As it happens, Ahaz is unconvinced, but today's preacher could explore why this might have been so. Going on, then, to any of the other three areas of the grid at the end of chapter 2, the preacher can ask questions which have infinitely more importance for my life than: 'Was Jesus born of a virgin and did Isaiah know about it?' If proof leapt out and hit me in the face on either of these matters, would my belief and behaviour be radically affected in any way?

But for the preacher to ask any or each of the questions: 'What echoes are there in the passage for me?', 'How has the passage been understood in the history of the church?' (and certainly there Jesus as 'God with us', together with the virgin birth does appear) and 'Does the passage offer a critique or confirmation to the contemporary world?' really is a worthwhile activity. If all we can do with these rich passages from Isaiah is play 'spot the text', why should the contemporary world – you and me included – be remotely interested? This example by no means rejects the uniqueness of the New Testament. Rather it seeks it out in terms of this great God of history being truly 'with us' in human form. The possibilities of interpretation are endless, but by using exegesis of the Old Testament to focus on the significance of 'Immanuel' for Isaiah we stand a chance of seeing the wood for the trees. We may, if we wish, emphasise the coming true element of Isaiah's prophecy for his day, as Syria and Israel were smashed by Assyria within seven or eight years. We may interpret other Old Testament assurances of 'Immanuel' (eg Isaiah 41:10) and we may go to the promise at the end of Matthew's gospel (28:20) and in Revelation 21:3. We may do just about anything, but whatever it is, to deserve the name of preaching, it should make a difference to the lives of the congregation, or at any rate have the potential to do so.

One of the culprits for deflecting the preacher from this sort of valuable exploration is surely the obsession with the future. Perhaps the cure is to recognise the difference between prediction and promise. This is true of many prophetic texts and the following examples – many of them drawn from Melugin's 'Isaiah and the worshipping community'[4] – demonstrate richer possibilities than Achtemeier's approach provides.

The first passage is Isaiah 9:6-7, immediately familiar to Christians in Advent services. In that context it immediately takes on a messianic significance. 'A child has been born for us, a son given to us. . . and there shall be endless peace for the throne of David and his kingdom' can hardly be heard by any Christian, even outside Advent, without seeing its fulfilment in Jesus. The preacher could well, if there is a sermon, raise questions about the 'original' meaning of these words and emphasise that they would make sense as one of a number of longings expressed in the Old Testament (sometimes worded as if they have already been fulfilled) for a king who would be a true representative of a just, righteous and peace-making God (compare Isaiah 11:1-9; Jeremiah 23:5-6). Though these passages do not use the term 'messiah', meaning 'anointed', they do hope for a king of the Davidic line, and all such kings were anointed. The passages are, in this sense messianic, even in pre-Christian history. It is this 'Jewish' history which Melugin thinks should be brought out clearly for the Christian worshipping community. He emphasises the way in which these words would have been read/heard by those editing the whole book of Isaiah. Already, they would mean something different from their 'original' meaning and, says Melugin, 'We should employ their hermeneutic method for our communities of faith.' (This may be compared to the point made earlier about redaction criticism and the editing of the book of Jeremiah.) The 'original' meaning of a passage is insufficient in itself for the Christian worshipping community. The question is not so much then: 'Did Isaiah or did he not predict Jesus, the Christian Messiah?' Even if the answer were definitively 'yes' when this question is asked of Isaiah 9:6-7, what difference would this make in our preaching?

If we concentrate on trying to represent accurately historical events or social institutions we are not being true to the primary interest of those who shaped the prophetic books. They were 'fundamentally concerned with using language performatively . . . to shape or transform the life of the faith community.'[5] So in Isaiah 7:14, as dealt with earlier, those responsible for the book of Isaiah in its present form were happy to take utterances concerning the Assyrian threat and use them in the context of the Babylonian exile two centuries later 'without explaining the differences between original meanings and later reinterpretation'.

The performative use of language, rather than the descriptive, also helps with other prophetic texts and later interpretation in the life of various faith communities. So the exhortation: '. . . defend the orphan, plead for the widow' (Isaiah 1:17) is meant, whether originally, in redaction or editing, or in Christian worship, not to explain something but rather to transform behaviour. Melugin compares this with the words: 'I pronounce you husband and wife' which 'create a marriage rather than explain a marriage'.

Similarly, prophetic statements about the future are not predictions which, like weather forecasts, are either accurate or inaccurate, but promises which are either fulfilled or unfulfilled and this in a whole range of ways at a whole range of times. Full objectivity about the 'original' meaning is, therefore, misguided. Interpretation and reinterpretation will always be shaped by the questions which the interpreters bring to the text.

Because of this it is quite acceptable for Christians in different periods to interpret texts typologically. It is not so much that each Old Testament figure should be taken as a New Testament 'type' (the traditional meaning of 'typology' between the two Testaments) as that experiences in the history of a worshipping community repeat themselves in some way or another. So Isaiah 49:8-12, 19-23; 60:4-9, 21 can be taken to apply to the Babylonian exile, and by Jews today to be extended to the return to Israel-Palestine. Christians, however, can relate them to a sort of spiritual exile in which they may be living now.[6]

We are much better placed, after these considerations, to judge what it is to preach the gospel to our own Christian community. Drawing on both the traditional and many of the more modern approaches to interpretation of the Old Testament, we are freed up to be part of an ongoing interpretation from within our own particular faith community. Melugin's observations are in line with modern Old Testament scholarship in looking at Isaiah 1-66 as a whole, instead of emphasising the separateness of 1-39; 40-55; 56-66, as was the predominant stress in the last century. Again, there are benefits to interpretation from both trends, but the thought that preaching might be consonant with the very interests and intentions of those who shaped the whole Isaianic corpus is encouraging as we seek to present the gospel.

Further Reading

J Barton, *Isaiah 1-39*, JSOT Press, Sheffield 1995.
G I Davies, *Hosea*, JSOT Press, Sheffield 1993.
R N Whybray, *The Second Isaiah*, JSOT Press, Sheffield 1983.

4

GETTING A HEARING

Long before the preacher begins the sermon, the degree of interest in an Old Testament text or theme will have been determined. A number of factors relating to the service as a whole will have a bearing. Whether a sense of worship has been cultivated and whether the congregation feels involved, for instance, are important, whatever the source or focus of the sermon. When it comes to preaching on the Old Testament, however, there is a particular need for very careful thought to be given to what leads up to the sermon. The choice of reading has been discussed in chapter 1. But even the most inspired choice will be to no avail if the actual reading does not make an impact. It may be argued that the inherent richness of the passage will be sufficient to get a good hearing. Experience suggests differently.

Sadly, many people come to the Old Testament in worship with some rather negative feelings. They may include any or even all the presuppositions mentioned in other chapters of this book: that the Old Testament is outdated, tedious, full of blood and gore or doom and gloom, packed with lists of unpronounceable names (strange that we are willing to tackle equally unfamiliar names in international sports events like the World Cup or the Olympic Games), and that it does not seem to have much to do with Jesus and even less to do with us.

Anyone trying to gain the attention of a listener who is predisposed to switch off knows that the first few seconds are crucial. When it comes to preaching on the Old Testament, these first few seconds are not those of the sermon, but those of the reading itself. Sometimes the opening words of the reading are themselves arresting, for example: 'Let me sing for my beloved my love-song concerning his vineyard . . .' (Isaiah 5:1) or 'King Belshazzar made a great festival for a thousand of his lords, and he was drinking wine in the presence of the thousand' (Daniel 5:1) or 'And the LORD sent Nathan to David. He came to him, and said to him . . .' (2 Samuel 12:1).

In the first case, the prophet himself has done the work for us. Isaiah imitated someone singing a ballad and we, like his original hearers, want to know how the story goes. He keeps our attention by the strange twists in the story and by the plays on words at its climax. In the second case, the passage itself sets the scene sufficiently vividly for us to want to know what happens. Even if we have never before heard of Belshazzar, we get the picture of quite a party going on and the feeling that something dramatic will happen. In the third case, we want to know what is said. However, this passage from 2 Samuel raises some interesting points about how a passage begins. It may be that it adds to the sense of intrigue to read the last part of the previous verse (from the previous chapter): 'But the things that David had done displeased the LORD.'

It is up to the preacher when choosing the version that is being read from to decide exactly where to start the passage. If someone else is doing the reading it is worth remembering the need to check which version is being used. Few preachers will have escaped the experience, especially when there is a readers' rota, of receiving a query, the day before (or worse the minute before) the service, about where the appointed passage begins or ends, since in the reader's version, the preacher's request seems to interrupt a verse. Worse still, is when a puzzled reader simply ploughs on without asking, because you the preacher must know what you are doing, even if you do seem to like beginning in the middle of a sentence! The precise delineation of the passage, including which version the preacher is expecting the congregation to hear, should not be left to chance.

The latter point is, of course, all the more vital should the sermon be taking a text in the traditional sense of one verse or a part of it. (The advantages and disadvantages of having a text will be considered below.) Disappointing is the experience when, even after a specific request for a particular version, the preacher suddenly finds everyone hearing words which send people off in a quite different direction from that of the precious text. The fact is that preaching on the Old Testament requires careful preparation, and not only by the preacher.

Returning to the passage from 2 Samuel, the further question arises of whether, 'But the thing that David had done displeased the LORD' is a satisfactory way to begin. After all, we should not assume that the listeners know what 'the thing' is. It is immensely off-putting in any gathering, no less in a church service, to have the feeling that everyone else knows something that you do not know. Surely, then, the preacher or whoever is introducing this reading from 2 Samuel needs to give some background.

However, my spirits droop when I hear someone say that we are going to be given the background. In an essay, this usually means that the writer is going to wait a few pages before getting round to addressing the precise question. In the introduction to a Bible reading, it generally involves a long narrative, usually in far less exciting form than the original Old Testament story itself. You probably know the experience of finding that when the reader eventually gets round to the reading itself you have lost all interest. And all this only goes to confirm what you already thought, namely, that the Old Testament is a boring volume, full of boring stories about boring people – and, worse still, that only boring people could possibly be engaged in listening to it – and you are one of them!

There is not necessarily a right or wrong way to begin a reading like the one about Nathan going to rebuke David. You may judge it best to go straight in or to offer a brief introduction. What is imperative, however, is that the preacher decides by thinking the whole thing through. The specific aim of the Old Testament sermon, its relation to the passage (I am assuming that there will always be one), and the movement of the service all need to be determined in advance. The preacher would do well to imagine what might help connect the congregation with the Old Testament in simple everyday English. For instance, a brief: 'So and so had been having some problems' or: 'We pick up the story at the point where . . .'.

On a particular broadcast of Choral Evensong on Radio 3, the Old Testament lesson was introduced simply with the words: 'A reading from the second book of Samuel'. This was perfect, as the reader gave me the source in a way that was quite sufficient, wasting absolutely no time before beginning the reading. It began: 'Now David was sitting between the two gates. The sentinel went up to the roof of the gate by the wall, and when he looked up, he saw a man running alone. The sentinel shouted and told the king. The king said, "If he is alone, there are tidings in his mouth." He kept coming, and drew near.' The second lesson was similarly introduced as 'A reading from the Acts of the Apostles'. It began: 'After they were released, they went to their friends and reported what the chief priests and the elders had said to them.'

Perhaps your preference would have been to have more information on both biblical readings. In the second lesson, for instance, the names of the 'they' would have helped and, indeed, this practice is suggested in the *Methodist Worship Book* (p 565). Perhaps you would also have preferred to have been given chapter and verse. I did, in fact, subsequently look this up in the *Radio Times*. But, for the service itself, I wanted to be addressed by the readings. Admittedly, there was no sermon on either reading but the readings were 'the Word' of this broadcast service. I was so glad that the first reader had not said: 'The second book of Samuel, chapter 18, beginning at verse 19 to chapter 19 verse 8a'. This is what the *Radio Times* told me. Interestingly, the broadcast reading did not begin at verse 19, as advertised, but at verse 24. Someone had clearly thought through not only the timing of the service (and we should not underestimate the importance of the length of the reading, even when we are not being broadcast), but also the nature of the opening verse. It was wise not to begin with: 'Then Ahimaaz son of Zadok said, "Let me run, and carry tidings to the king that the LORD has delivered him from the power of his enemies." The other opening was far more arresting.

What, I wonder, would have been the difference in the effect of the reading if it had been introduced with a full chapter and verse announcement? There is also the tradition to give this in the form of: 'The 19th verse of the 18th chapter of the 2nd book of Samuel'. This is a particularly frustrating practice for those who, whether listening to a radio broadcast or sitting in the pew, want to follow the reading in their own Bibles. They cannot begin to locate the book until the third part of the announcement, by which time the reading is beginning and they then cannot remember the chapter, let alone the verse.

I have laboured this point about introducing the Old Testament reading because I believe that it can help or hinder us in getting a hearing for our Old Testament preaching. We have to make considerable efforts to win attention when we know that many will be inclined to switch off at the very mention of the Old Testament. Television advertisers have to work hard to stop viewers from going to put the kettle on and to win attention for a product, especially one which has been long on the go. How much more do we as preachers, lacking the visual stimulus of the screen, have to think carefully about the precise needs of our listeners as our reading begins, and work hard at producing the words which will best meet these needs.

There is probably no one rule, and variety may well be the spice of worship. To my mind, the best way to introduce our example from 2 Samuel about David and Nathan is to emulate the cited Choral Evensong practice and say simply: 'A reading from the second book of Samuel'. If congregations are provided with Bibles, they may be given the page number. If they have copies of the notice sheet with the service's readings on it, they can check the details on this. If they have no such information and they want to check the reading when they get home, they can surely ask the preacher at the end. All I am advocating is a certain professionalism in how we, as preachers, endeavour to prepare the way for a sermon on the Old Testament. If, in the present example, what David has done wrong has importance for what we are going to say in the sermon or if, in any instance, we feel that one piece of information is vital for making sense of the passage, then let us give it briefly and in a way which arouses, rather than kills, interest in what is to follow.

Some very useful tips are offered in books by David Schlafer.[1] Though he is writing largely about the wording and shaping of the sermon itself, some of what he says applies also to the readings. For instance, do not give away the plot; otherwise the congregation has no incentive to listen. (See below on telling stories in chapter 7.)

Another incentive to listen, of course, is not to announce the details of the reading at all, but simply begin. This is worth trying, especially with words so powerful as those of much of the Old Testament. No one with a Bible to hand is likely then to spend time trying to find the reading. Furthermore, a reading heard is a very different thing from a reading read 'to yourself' which is essentially what happens if you follow the passage in your copy of the Bible. We are sometimes urged: 'Let us hear the word of God!' Yes, let us hear it!

The Old Testament characters themselves were adept at getting a hearing. We see this best where prophets were concerned. Essentially spokesmen, the prophets had to devise strategies for gaining attention especially if what they were going to say was going to be unpopular. Nathan himself does it in our example in 2 Samuel 12. Rather than laying into David, he tells him a story. The king then incriminates himself.

A similar example comes in the Isaiah 5 passage mentioned earlier. The prophet's hearers, like most people, are keen to hear a tale. To keep attention until the very end, there is an additional technique. This is a play on words in verse 7, where the 'justice' and 'righteousness' for which God looks sound, in Hebrew, very like the 'bloodshed' and a 'cry' which he, in fact, gets from his people. This may get lost in English translation, though some have attempted to capture it. There is nothing to stop us devising our own careful choice of words to get this, or any other crucial point, across. It may be objected that the preacher's job is not to be clever with words, but to preach the word of God to his people. If those whom God chose in ancient Israel (or in first century Palestine, for that matter, including Jesus himself) knew the value of carefully chosen words, style, and structure, it is hard to see how we can dispense with such efforts. The medium is (vital to) the message.

Whether in their pithy introductions (some as brief as 'Listen!'), or in their more crafted techniques, the prophets remind us that communication involves careful preparation. It is often said that the preacher may be comforted when it becomes apparent that someone has valued an inadequate sermon or that the preacher may not know the effects of the sermon (which may, of course, be an advantage!). True though these statements may be, the choice of words and the length of our introduction to the Old Testament reading and to the sermon itself may play a role in whether or not we preach the gospel that day.

Not only how we begin but how we end a reading can also make a difference. 'May the Lord add his blessing to the reading of his word' always seems so unnecessary when a striking passage has been clearly and arrestingly read. We should practise beforehand reading out loud, raising questions of the reading or, as Schlafer puts it, 'talk with the text', asking questions such as: 'Where did this come from?'; 'What's at stake here?' We must get a feel for the language and the types of speech. Form-critical issues emerge here. Commentaries tell us, for example, that Amos 5:2 imitates a funeral dirge and that Isaiah 1:2-9, like many other prophetic oracles, imitates a court case. Imagine that! A little imagination may go a long way to setting the scene and getting a hearing for a later point in Old Testament preaching.

We should think carefully too how the last phrase of the reading will sound to the hearers. There are some good and pertinent responses suggested in the *Methodist Worship Book*. Even 'Thanks be to God', however, may be better avoided. I once heard it after the devastating words: 'Peter went out and wept bitterly.' It wrecked the effect, especially as the wonderfully evocative aria, 'Have mercy, Lord, on me' from Bach's *St Matthew Passion* had been chosen to follow on immediately, as in the oratorio itself. 'Thanks be to God' sounds even worse after 'Judas went out and hanged himself'! We would not dream of adding some extra phrase after the recital of a Shakespearean sonnet. The poem says it all. So, more often than not, does the biblical reading, especially when it is of Old Testament poetry.

Turning to the sermon itself, we need to consider the effect of having a text. You may well know the wonderfully funny sketch from *Beyond the Fringe*, recorded by Alan Bennett. In printed form, it is entitled 'Take a Pew' and is introduced: 'The 29th verse of the 14th chapter of the book of Genesis'. In another version of this sketch, the source is announced as 'the 1st verse of the 14th chapter of the 2nd book of Kings'. This in itself sends up the sort of convoluted announcement of the reading which we discussed earlier. There is, incidentally, no such verse, as Genesis 14 ends at verse 24, but the text which follows does exist. It is: 'But my brother Esau is an hairy man, but I am a smooth man.' After a strange emphasis on 'I' as this text is repeated, Alan Bennett then makes no further reference to the text itself until the very end of the sermon. What comes in between these two renditions of the text bears absolutely no relation to it. Moreover, the 'sermon' is full of distorted, contrived, and artificially 'trendy' phrases and illustrations.

Equally off-putting in introducing the Old Testament reading or sermon is the use of antiquated phrases. Why do people so often speak of Moses or Elijah or any other Old Testament figure as 'going forth'? I have never gone forth anywhere myself. I have just gone – and so have Moses and Elijah. Surely, when we refer in our sermon to Moses on Sinai, 'Moses went . . .' is more recognisable than 'Moses went forth . . .'. 'Went forth' somehow makes the Old Testament sound very old – if not positively weary.

The opposite of using the text merely as a peg to hang a sermon on (repeated merely at the beginning and the end) is to kill the text by overdoing it. I vividly recall being in a tiny Lakeland chapel many years ago (it had better remain nameless just in case the preacher happens to be reading this book – highly unlikely though that is!). Every minute or so the preacher repeated his text. It happened to be from the New Testament, but the experience would have been just as comical had it been from the Old Testament. I got to the point where I dreaded it coming. But – I still remember the text! Indeed, there was no forgetting it!

Considered, even practised, repetition of a text may, however, be supremely effective. A past master of this was the late James S Stewart, former Moderator of the General Assembly of the Church of Scotland and Professor of New Testament at the University of Edinburgh. It is his Old Testament texts that I remember so vividly from hearing him preach as long ago as 1973-76. In his case, I remember some of what went with the texts, so they obviously worked. An arresting text, perhaps because of its use of language, particularly if it is used sparingly as a sort of refrain to remind the congregation of the key issue at the beginning or end of each section of the sermon, may, indeed, help to get a hearing for the Old Testament.

Colin Morris advocates preaching on what he calls 'the big texts' because they take us into the big themes of our faith.[2] He tells of another great Scottish preacher's reply to the question whether there was any biblical text that he regretted not preaching on more frequently. The nineteenth century Thomas Chalmers replied: 'Yes, "Comfort, comfort ye my people, saith your God." '

We should, urges Colin Morris, be more concerned with preaching these big texts than with worrying about the fact that we may not be highly original. Amusingly, he recalls sermons (not his own!) where the chosen text was particularly bizarre, including: 'Now Rachel had taken the household gods . . . and sat on them' (Genesis 31:34); '. . . the fourth river is the Euphrates' (Genesis 2:14 – this one sounds quite promising to me, but I should perhaps resolve right now never to try it!), and 'God appointed a worm . . .' (Jonah 4:7). Perhaps this is rather a desperate way of getting a hearing, as fellow preachers and congregations cry in puzzled admiration: 'What on earth can he or she possibly make of that?'

Many great Old Testament texts have the feel of having spoken to people of faith long before us. Sometimes, of course, we are disappointed by the loss of a much-loved translation. The preacher's 'substitute' spoils this sense for us. A well-known example is the opening verses of Psalm 121: 'I lift my eyes to the hills – from where will my help come? My help comes from the LORD, who made heaven and earth.' Older versions punctuate this differently so that it reads as if the psalmist draws his inspiration from the hills themselves. It is there that he finds God. Though the former may be the more accurate rendering of the Hebrew, the latter also has 'true meaning' for many people. Both renderings have sustained people over the centuries. There are, after all, many different ways of getting a hearing.

Further Reading

A G Auld, *Amos*, JSOT Press, Sheffield 1986.
James L Crenshaw, *Trembling at the Threshold of a Biblical Text*, Eerdmans, Grand Rapids 1994. This is an excellent collection of short sermons by an Old Testament scholar, based variously on Old Testament texts alone, New Testament texts alone, and often on a combination of Old and New Testament texts.
John Eaton, *Interpreted by Love: Expositions of 40 Great Old Testament Passages*, Bible Reading Fellowship, Oxford 1994.

Other examples of sermons, including ones on Old Testament texts, are printed in each volume of Fellowship Papers of the College of Preachers, available to members. The sermons come from a wide range of preachers.

5

BEGINNING WITH GOD

Most if not all preaching is in the context of worship. I am afraid that when the first words are 'Good morning' or even 'Welcome to worship' my heart sinks. For me, they immediately direct attention to the person leading the worship and it somehow takes me longer to remember why I have come. I am unfortunately reminded of Bruce Forsyth's: 'Nice to see you. To see you nice.' I much prefer a call to worship which reminds me that 'in the beginning God . . .'. Simply: 'Let us worship God' will do. As Crenshaw says to his congregation in a sermon entitled 'A stairway to heaven': 'You did not come here to hear a brilliant sermon, to listen to uplifting music, to be entertained, or to greet a friend after the service. No, a hundred times no. You came here because you believe in the possibility of linking your life with God, who gave you life in the beginning.'[1] Though I cannot help feeling that it is not always such a clear choice between God, the music, or the friend, I am convinced by Crenshaw's words: 'You – yes, we – have come because we desire above everything else to encounter the living God, and we dare to expose our lives to the searching gaze of the eternal Judge.'

This sermon is based on Genesis 11:1-9 with its conclusion that 'Therefore it [the place] was called Babel, because there the LORD confused the language of all the earth . . .'. Crenshaw warns: 'Make no mistake about it. God's entrance into our lives is no laughing matter. In Jewish tradition, three men managed to scale that ladder to heaven and gazed upon God's face. One died, another went mad, and the third lived to tell about it.' He concludes:

'Confronting ultimate mystery, let us be silent and marvel at the confusion God brings. Perhaps then we can bow down and worship before the mystery that lets itself be glimpsed from afar. Then and only then can we experience the power of Pentecost that turned this story upside down.' [2]

I would argue that just as Babel must precede Pentecost (Acts of the Apostles 2), so Sinai must precede Bethlehem (Matthew 2; Luke 2). How can we possibly begin to wonder at the incarnation if we have not first read Exodus 19? And there God says to Moses not: 'Good morning and welcome to Sinai!' but – well, what does God say? It is hard to put thunder, lightning and trumpet blast into words but as a result 'all the people who were in the camp trembled' (verse 16).

It is here that we find the most imperative reason of all for preaching on the Old Testament. It is not only that we would be pretty well baffled if we erased all Old Testament echoes and quotations from the New Testament and, in particular, the Infancy Narratives. It is that unless we begin to get some sense of this awesome God and 'take our shoes off' when on holy ground (Exodus 3:5 – again on Horeb-Sinai), the immensity of his revelation in a human life will completely pass us by.

Worship must begin with and centre on God. It is not a matter simply of substituting the word 'God' for the word 'Jesus'. Refrains of 'God, we love you' could be as inane as refrains of 'Jesus, we love you.' It is not a matter simply of whether we go in for this sort of song. It is whether real content is given in the rest of the worship, besides the singing, to the word 'Jesus' ('saviour') in terms of God himself and to what it might mean to 'love' him. It is sometimes suggested that the only places of worship in Great Britain where attendance is not dwindling markedly are those where 'I love Jesus' is the constant refrain. The implication is sometimes drawn that we should not complicate matters with too much theology. If there is any truth in what Crenshaw says attracts his people regularly to church, it is surely not too much but too little theology which is dangerous. How we make our entire worship theocentric, as was Jesus' and Paul's, are questions for books other than this one, including some planned for this series, *The Preacher's Library*. This book's concern is how we communicate this theology by drawing on the huge scope of the Old Testament.

The Old Testament is not a systematic theology. If we treat it as such we run the risk, not for the first time in Old Testament study, of pressing all its writers into one mould, of reducing what they communicate to concepts. Even such grand concepts as love and holiness seem somehow to miss the thrust of the writers' efforts. These writers seem rather to be concerned with the entire being of God and then with the religious life of a community, and of individuals within it. Those behind the Old Testament are concerned with the great breadth of God and then the great breadth of humanity. Only in this context does their concentration on 'a people of God' begin to make sense. (See chapter 6.)

The two prophetic books which in their respective ways most emphasise the holiness of God are Isaiah and Ezekiel. It is no accident that it is in these books that we also find an emphasis on God's being present with his people for the world. We saw a few of the many occurrences in Isaiah 1-39 in chapter 2 and more examples from Isaiah in chapter 3, but Isaiah 55, particularly verses 3-5, provides a clear example. A similar promise of a peaceful and lasting Davidic covenant occurs in Ezekiel 37:24-27. It is striking that shortly before the immensely detailed vision of the Temple (40-46) we find the words: 'My dwelling place shall be with them; and I will be their God, and they shall be my people. Then the nations shall know that I the LORD sanctify Israel, when my sanctuary is among them forevermore' (37:27-28).

The Old Testament directs attention not so much to theological concepts which we can arrange under neat headings, but to the activity of God, variously as creator, king, father, redeemer, and supremely as saviour. This last title for God cannot be overemphasised, especially when it comes to preaching on the Old Testament in the context of Christian worship. The saving God is praised in Psalm 68 (eg verse 20) and appealed to 'to do his stuff' in many psalms of lament (eg 69:1).

The different types of psalms and their settings in life began to attract considerable attention early in the twentieth century. The appropriateness of their current life setting, especially in worship as distinct from private devotion, has become more recently the subject of much debate. The psalms of lament, with their doubts and complaints to God, will be considered in the last chapter of this book as their writers, in some way, try 'making sense of experience'. (There are also similarities between such psalms and the complaints in the books of Job and Jeremiah.) At this point, however, some other aspects of the use of psalms in worship and in preaching will be considered.

It has been argued that songs in the Old Testament – chiefly though not exclusively in the book of Psalms – should not be expounded in worship but simply left to perform their original function of addressing God. We ought, therefore, 'to pray them and sing them rather than preach them'.[3] Though recognising the unique value of the Psalms (as shown in the historic place of the entire psalter in Matins and Evensong in the Church of England and their increasing use by other denominational traditions) as worship in themselves, I judge following this advice an unnecessary deprivation. Whilst acknowledging Gowan's warning about pedestrianising the lyrical form of the Psalms by our weaker efforts, I wonder about the huge gaps in our theology which might ensue from not preaching on any of the Psalms which address God.

Of course, you do not have to preach on a text for it to say something. Evidence the way in which hymns, based on the Psalms, have long been used to convey what might be called the 'creed' of the people of Israel. The metrical psalms particularly favoured by the Church of Scotland (eg 'Ye gates lift up your heads on high', based on Psalm 24:7-10 and 'All people that on earth do dwell', based on Psalm 100) and many great hymns of Charles Wesley and Isaac Watts convey the faith of the psalmists. Isaac Watts' 'Sweet is the work, my God, my king', based on Psalm 92 and superbly his 'I'll praise my Maker while I've breath', based on Psalm 146, illustrate this. Do I have to choose between hearing such psalms as sung in these hymns or as sung by the choristers of Canterbury Cathedral? Do I have to choose between either of these and Gelineau settings, or these psalms as simply read – and then from which version? Following this line to its logical conclusion, I might not be allowed to benefit at all from these psalms, or any others for that matter, unless I read or chant them in the original Hebrew to be sure that I have not damaged them.

And how am I to enjoy verses 1, 2, and 4 of Psalm 84 as famously set by Brahms in *Ein deutsches Requiem*, beginning 'Wie lieblich sind dein Wohnungen, Herr Zebaoth!'? It may be of interest to note that in the same work Brahms also sets Psalms 126:5,6 and 39:4-7. In fact, alongside snippets of James, John, Hebrews, 1 Corinthians and Revelation from the New Testament, it is worth remarking that the Old Testament makes up the rest of the libretto, drawing on Isaiah 40:6-8 (though programme notes to hand misinform me that 1 Peter 1:24-25 is its origin); Isaiah 35:10; 66:13, not to mention Ecclesiasticus 51:27 (the same programme notes confuse it with Ecclesiastes – obviously a bad day for the note-writer!) and the Wisdom of Solomon 3:1 from the Apocrypha. Does it make any difference whether I hear or sing this as in the Lutheran Bible, as Brahms set it, or in English – neither, after all, the language of the psalmist? As we saw in chapter 4, the translation does matter and a poor one, whether in terms of accuracy or of poetic features, may well spoil the psalm. It does not need a sermon to do that!

Gowan's point is predominantly that one of the benefits of the form-critical approach to the Bible is that preachers should be challenged by the 'beauty, pathos and power of the Psalter and all the rest of Hebrew poetry, to find new ways of bringing some of that into the words of their sermons'. He admits too that there are parts of psalms which are eminently preachable. But his distinction between those which cannot be preached, namely words addressed to God (that is, prayer, which praises or protests to God) and those which can, namely recitals of what God is like and what he does, appears not only artificial, but very hard to carry through into the integrity of the Psalms themselves.

Now, as then, the Psalms are designed to cultivate worship, with a whole gamut of human emotions coming into play. The resources of the Psalms are available to the preacher and let us not limit them to Psalms 23 and 139. Admittedly, there are in the Psalms, as elsewhere in the Old Testament, verses better not preached on. There are certainly emotions in the Psalms which are not to be recommended. Psalm 137:7-9 is often cited as particularly offensive. But even this vindictiveness, as also found in Jeremiah, could perhaps be allowed to surface in our preaching, if only to recognise the honesty and naturalness of its causes in human experience then and now. In this case, the words are probably better preached on than recited or, even worse, sung with relish especially in the respectable setting of Choral Evensong! I am still left wondering, however, why what could be brought to God in the prayer of the Jerusalem Temple cannot similarly be brought in Canterbury Cathedral.

I am not sure that the answer to this is the one which the Old Testament detractors might well offer, namely that we (human beings) have progressed from such dark feelings and thoughts. What may be all right for Jews, at least for biblical ones, is not acceptable to Christians seems to be the implication. It is, however, obvious from the hymns of Wesley and Watts that both men were steeped in Old and New Testaments alike and moved easily from one to the other. They clearly assume that the faith of the church is continuous with the faith of ancient Israel. So these writers, when dealing with Old Testament echoes or quotations, especially from the Psalms, slip easily into Christological mode. Wesley, for instance, in the hymn: 'My heart is full of Christ and longs its glorious matter to declare!' takes phrase after phrase from Psalm 45, a royal wedding hymn, adapts it, and applies it to Jesus, risen and ascended. Whilst there may be the risk in this of Christianising to the point of departing from what the psalm could have meant to its singers BC, there is merit in its declaration that the God of the church is all of a piece with the God of Israel.

This last point is important, not least because of an untruth perpetuated by Christians who mention the Old Testament in passing only to denigrate it and who thereby demonstrate that they have not actually read or heard it. As a Christian, I do not take kindly to people telling me that things are in the New Testament when they are not, especially when they are supposed to pertain to the God I worship. A Jew similarly should not have to listen to someone telling him or her about aspects of God in the Hebrew Bible which reveal that this someone has missed out great chunks, if not all, of it. Now since this Hebrew Bible forms the Christian's Old Testament, it is incumbent on the Christian not to misrepresent it.

The most common instance of this in my experience is the assertion in Christian worship that Jesus taught love of God and love of neighbour. So far, so good. The trouble starts when the corollary is, sometimes only hinted but more often than not stated, that this was a new idea and that without Jesus we should have had no idea that the essence of the biblical religion was love of God and love of neighbour. Sometimes, this misapprehension is partly corrected by remembering that the command to love God first occurs in Deuteronomy 6:5, at the heart of Jesus' law as a Jew. Far more rarely is the second misapprehension corrected by recognising that Jesus quotes the second part of his summary of the law (Matthew 22:37-40) from Leviticus 19:18, part of the holiness code (see next chapter).

That the writer of the programme notes for a performance of Brahms' *German Requiem* does not recognise that Isaiah and not 1 Peter originated the words: 'All flesh is grass . . . but the word of our God shall stand forever' is bad enough. For the Christian preacher to suggest that Jesus invented love of neighbour is far more culpable. It is something far more serious than Isaianic or Levitical copyright. It makes the Old Testament say what we want it to say. We decide beforehand what it says about God, rather than entertaining the possibility that God may say something in and through it that we have not fully grasped.

In the entire Old Testament, love of God and love of neighbour are assumed to belong together. Why else should ill-treatment of neighbour be so vehemently condemned at every point (eg Micah 2:2), especially when it is combined with apparent worship of God, as in Micah 6:6-8; Hosea 6:6; Isaiah 1:10-17; Amos 5:21-24? 'See the blatant contradiction' is what all these prophets, and others, are saying. How else does one give practical content to this 'love of God' and make any sort of worship, be it hymns, prayers, festivals and holy days, or sacrifice acceptable to God?

Another common Christian misrepresentation of the Old Testament is to concede, rather grudgingly: 'Maybe then, the people of eighth century Israel and Judah, and the originators of Deuteronomy and Leviticus, did believe in treating your neighbour well.' But they then continue: 'The thing was that by neighbour they meant only their fellow-Israelite.' The whole question of Old Testament attitudes to 'foreigners' is a complex one. It is not the same at all times and in all places. Joshua, Ruth, Ezra and Isaiah (taken as a whole even more so), to mention just a few, throw up a whole range of potentially and perhaps realistically contradictory views.

In the Old Testament, God is intimately involved with human beings – even if it means bloodthirsty victory over your enemy. There is no getting away from the horror of passages like 'The Moabites shall be trodden down in their place as straw is trodden down in a dung-pit' (Isaiah 25:10b) though, as with Psalm 137:7-9, we need not feel obliged to preach on it. We cannot erase from the record: 'When my angel goes in front of you, and brings you to the Amorites, the Hittites, the Perizzites, the Canaanites, the Hivites, and the Jebusites, and I blot them out' (Exodus 23:23). But neither should the end of the sentence, with its demand on the Israelites for loyalty to their God, be overlooked: 'you shall not bow down to their gods, or worship them, or follow their practices, but you shall utterly demolish them and break their pillars in pieces' (verse 24). After all, who do you judge to be God's enemies in the Second World War or Bosnia or Kosovo, especially if you happen to have belonged or to belong to a particular ethnic or religious group? This is not to go along with the all too common view that the God of the Old Testament is a God of vengeance who gives us a free hand to be as brutal as we like. It is to remind ourselves that this is one part of the all too human perception of God by 'tribal groups' of any time and place. (See further chapter 7.) We are not permitted to conclude from a limited reading that the Old Testament knows nothing of love. As preachers at any rate, we are charged to think before we speak. We do not talk about the New Testament off the top of our heads, so why talk about the Old Testament like that?

Neglect the Old Testament and the preacher and congregation will not just fail to understand the New Testament but will positively misunderstand it. They will fill it with modern prejudices, separating the spiritual from the physical, the philosophical from the historical, and probably other distortions. In this, they may resemble the second century heretic, Marcion, who rejected not only the entire Old Testament as presenting an unacceptable God but also the incarnation of the creator God. We should beware individualising the religion of the New Testament into something cosy. As I recently heard the immensely effective preacher, David Day, put it (in a sermon on Emmaus), we should resist representing Christianity as: 'Tea for two and two for tea. Me for Jesus; Jesus for me.' There is fierce judgement in the New Testament, notably from Jesus himself (see Matthew 25).

Beginning with God is a real need not just in our preaching but in our entire worship, all that goes into it and all that flows out of it. Why in order to stress love and grace in the New Testament should we run down the Old? Why should we imagine that the God of the New Testament is in competition with himself? If the Bible's theology is not systematic, no less is it steadily progressive, as was at one time believed. Its whole mode of revelation is not primarily the imparting of abstract ideas which become the more acceptable, the later the period. Rather it is a testimony to what God has done for and with his people.

This alerts us to the other false contrast often drawn between Old and New Testaments. In the Old, it is said, we find a God who first demands obedience and who then bestows his favour on his people. Nothing is clearer from the book of Deuteronomy alone that the New lies in line with the Old in that God's grace comes first (7:7-9). His love for his people, which is totally unmerited, is given as the sole reason for his singling them out. In both presentations of 'the Ten Commandments' (in Deuteronomy 5 and Exodus 20), God's saving his people from slavery is given as the motive for their obedience. (See next chapter.)

The Old Testament gives us not only the medium but also the grounds for worship. Its books are not an optional, but an essential, part of our scripture. Only when we have been with Moses on Sinai, as it were, can we get the message of: 'And the Word became flesh and lived among us, and we have seen his glory, the glory as of a father's only son, full of grace and truth' (John 1:14). We need to keep beginning with God in Christian worship because then and only then will we get the big idea and the big picture. Only at this point should we tackle the big text of 'the Word became flesh . . . full of grace and truth.' To conclude this chapter very much in the vein in which it began, it has been said of preaching that the lasting impression which it should leave in the congregation's mind is not that they have heard a great sermon but that they have been shown a great God. The Old Testament offers assistance to do this which is simply not available anywhere else. With its huge perspective, there is nothing like it to enlarge our grasp of God.

Further Reading

Much useful information on the relationship between the book of Psalms and the worshipping community is offered in the following volumes:

Walter Brueggemann, *The Psalms and the Life of Faith*, Fortress Press, Minneapolis 1995.
J Day, *Psalms*, JSOT Press, Sheffield 1990.
John H Eaton, *The Psalms Come Alive*, Mowbray, Oxford 1984
Claus Westermann, *The Living Psalms*, T&T Clark, Edinburgh 1989.

A very helpful examination of many aspects of prayer in the Old Testament is to be found in Robert Davidson's *The Courage to Doubt*, SCM Press, London 1983, and in Michael E W Thompson's *I Have Heard Your Prayer*, Epworth Press, Peterborough 1996 and, though more technically and expensively, in Samuel E Balentine's *Prayer in the Hebrew Bible*, Fortress Press, Minneapolis 1993. In all three volumes, the thought is that the Psalms and many other Old Testament books have something to teach a modern community of faith about spirituality.

6

BEING THE PEOPLE OF GOD

The Old Testament reading suggested in *The Methodist Worship Book* for the ordination of presbyteral ministers is Isaiah 6:1-8. The passage ends with the word of commitment from the newly-cleansed prophet: 'Here am I; send me!' It is a pity that the next verse is not included, for it is this verse which gives the commission from God: 'Go and say to this people!' Immediately, we are aware of the vital context of the prophet's ministry. Without God's people, the prophet would be talking to himself. So, by extension, would the newly-ordained minister and so would any Christian preacher.

It may be a pity, but it is certainly no wonder, that verse 9 is not included in the lectionary reading, as what might appear bright, invigorating words of commission: 'Go and say . . .' are immediately followed by some of the most discouraging words you could ever give to a potential preacher. The prophet has to say 'to this people': 'Keep listening, but do not comprehend; keep looking, but do not understand.' Verse 10 gets worse with: 'Make the mind of this people dull, and stop their ears, and shut their eyes, so that they may not look with their eyes, and listen with their ears, and comprehend with their minds, and turn and be healed.' It may be remarked that the lectionary for Year C's Principal Service on the 5th Sunday in Ordinary time is braver and indicates that verses 9-13 may be added to the reading of Isaiah 6:1-8.

Is not this just the sort of passage that causes the Christian immense trouble with the Old Testament? In the first instance, it is puzzling. Why should the messenger have such a negative task? In the second instance, it hints at a rather unpleasant God, one who fears that 'this people' might understand the message, presumably one of rebuke, and consequently repent. What sort of God could possibly prefer people not to 'be healed'?

The obvious answer is the one given so readily by disparagers of the Old Testament generally, namely, that the Old Testament's God is vindictive and destructive. No wonder we concentrate on the New Testament where, the patter continues, it emerges that God loves his people after all. We saw in the previous chapter that this distinction between the God of the Old and the God of the New Testaments is a false one, but since 'testament' means 'covenant' and a covenant involves more than one party, the question follows: is the distinction Christians make by not attending to the Old Testament similarly false? What are preachers, in particular, actually saying when they neglect to preach on the Old Testament? And what presuppositions are their congregations accepting by being content not to hear it preached? If the covenant between God and his people instituted at Sinai is somehow related to the covenant between God and his people instituted in the upper room – and the New Testament writers certainly think it is – then we simply cannot afford not to explore the connection.

In this chapter, I want to raise many of the questions as found on the grid in chapter 2. (An exercise might be to fill in the grid taking Isaiah 6:1-10 as the centre.) The aim is to urge, if not compel, all Christian preachers to preach on the Old Testament. Certainly, the argument of compulsion will loom large in this chapter, not least because in Isaiah 6 we find compulsion being what drives him on to preach in the first place. (Whether chapter 6 represents the initial call of the prophet or a later commission is not agreed by commentators and is immaterial to our argument.) A sense of compulsion is a feature common to the Old Testament prophets (eg Jeremiah 15:17; 20:9) and to Christian preachers down the ages, including those of the twenty-first century. It is hard to imagine anyone taking on the task otherwise.

Biblical references in this chapter will be dominated by the prophetic books, including Isaiah. The reason for this is not only as a possible corrective to the view of prophecy as prediction, so beloved of those who use the prophets as a happy hunting-ground for predictions of New Testament or even present-day events, but also because it is the prophets, alongside the books of the law, which spell out, in practical terms, what it is for a people to 'love God'. Admittedly individuals, usually kings, are sometimes addressed by prophets (eg David by Nathan, Ahab by Elijah, Ahaz by Isaiah, Zedekiah by Jeremiah). Predominantly, however, it is a whole people which is addressed. The identity of 'this people' in 'Old Testament times', and today, constitutes the central focus of this chapter.

In Isaiah 6 alone, the word 'people' occurs four times. Isaiah identifies with 'a people' unworthy of God (verse 5). In our crucial verse, he is commanded to speak to 'this people' (verse 9). Thereby he has to deaden the response of 'this people' (verse 10) until their consequent punishment leaves all the houses of the land 'without people' (verse 11).

The word immediately before 'people' is often significant, and not only in Isaiah 6. We have seen, in chapter 3, how the message of Hosea has been reinterpreted by Elizabeth Achtemeier as addressed to the church. Even if not all preachers could follow her approach and method of relating Old and New Testament texts, all have to decide whether or not they believe that the Old Testament is addressed to the 'people of Israel' as constituted by the Christian community. It may be noted, even in a book written out of and for Christian commitment, that 'the people of Israel' as constituted by the Jewish community still exists today. The downright inaccurate view that Jews exist today only as the forerunners of Christians and the genuinely debatable view that the Jewish covenant has been superseded by that inaugurated by Christ – technically known as 'supersessionism' – are both rejected by this author.

When it comes to Isaiah 6, there are certainly puzzling features in the Hebrew. For example, we do not normally find 'this' before 'people'. It has been suggested that perhaps the term (occurring in both verses 9 and 10) expresses contempt for the people, a people who seem incapable of grasping what Isaiah is trying to say. It certainly sounds far more distant than 'my people' or even 'the people' or even 'a people'.

Some commentators attempt to make sense of the verses about deafening and blinding by saying that what they are describing is not the purpose of Isaiah's ministry but the result. After all, inflicting such disabilities is the opposite of what prophets are normally expected to do (eg Isaiah 35:5). However, the thought that, in retrospect, Isaiah concludes that the more he speaks the less people listen is hardly comforting. Nonetheless, it is true that the more a message is declared the more chance there is for it not to be heard. Either in advance or with hindsight, the prophet may realise this.

'Go and say to this people' may then be considered a particularly uncomfortable sub-title for a book designed to encourage preaching on the Old Testament. But I choose it advisedly. Not only does it sum up what we are called to do, in words addressed to an Old Testament prophet, but it raises the question, especially in the context of the whole of Isaiah 6, what precisely we think we are doing by preaching at all? Do we believe that through us God addresses his people? Do we believe that the Christian church, of which we are a part, is still specifically addressed as God's people? The questions repay close, considered and constant attention. The prophet variously gives hope, courage, warning. As we bring to bear any number of the questions from the preparation for preaching grid, in what sense, if any, do we believe that scripture is actually addressed to us now? As we move from text to sermon, in what way are we moving from asking what it meant to what it means?

When I see a list of questions instead of a series of statements, I tend to conclude that the writer does not know what he or she is talking about. It is hoped that all the questions of the previous paragraph will not be so construed. Rather the intention is to ask every reader to come to an honest conclusion in answer to each question and crucially to the one: 'Which people is being addressed?' – by Isaiah and by all the Old Testament writers? Does 'this people' include us? This is the crucial question, not only of this chapter, but of the whole of this book; hence its sub-title.

If we swallow the 'old' angry God of the Old Testament line, we can be excused for rejecting the 'old' ideas of the Old Testament addressed to an 'old' people, angry and vindictive like their God, and belonging to an 'old' covenant. But, as we have seen in the previous chapter, this option is not available to any Christian genuinely listening not only to the Old Testament but also to the New. The new covenant in which individuals will know God's law and want to keep it is still a communal covenant (Jeremiah 31:33).

It is on the new covenant passage in the book of Jeremiah that the New Testament draws (eg Hebrews 8:8-12; 10:16-17). In Jeremiah 31 the 'covenant formula' occurs as the hope for the future: 'and I will be their God, and they shall be my people' (Jeremiah 31:33). Similarly in Ezekiel we find at the heart of a passage about a new covenant (34:25-31) the hope that: 'They shall know that I, the LORD their God, am with them, and that they, the house of Israel, are my people.' This formula, recurrent in various forms in such a wide spread of Old Testament literature, is also implied in Isaiah 6. In its most terse formulation, 'my people; your God', it occurs in Isaiah 40:1.

Let us not get bogged down here with the question of whether we are the only people, though we should at times address the matter of other faiths in our preaching. We need at this point to concentrate on the question: 'Are we counted amongst God's people?' Are we listening or might we have become 'this people' as distinct from 'his people' in a way we do not intend or desire? Like Isaiah's contemporaries, we are not being addressed because we are not listening.

Christians sometimes think that with the question of fulfilment it is all or nothing. As we saw in chapter 3, however, fulfilment is not quite so simple. That some elements of Jeremiah 31:31-34 have been fulfilled in Jewish history in terms not shared by Christians, whilst others have been fulfilled in Christian history in terms not shared by Jews, is certainly a possibility. The key question for Christians is surely not how God's covenant stands with Jews, but how God's covenant, old, new or renewed stands with us. (We may note Paul's wrestling with the logic of all this in Romans 9-11.) The claim of Christian worship, notably in the words from 1 Corinthians 11:25 which we use in the Eucharist, is that the covenant tradition has been passed on to us. Whatever it is that is newly invested by Jesus in the concept of covenant (see Matthew 26:26-29; Luke 22:17-20), it is not the communal. That has always been there in his scriptures (our Old Testament) and still is in ours (Old and New Testaments).

Preaching is always a communal matter. The community is admittedly made up of individuals, but sermons are addressed to the people of God and to individuals only in so far as they claim membership of the people of God. We are never preached to alone – unless congregations have dwindled even more than we are led to believe! Even if I am alone physically, as when listening to a service on the radio or television, I am not hearing a private address. It is no accident that we do not have sermons for one! God's word is mediated to us alongside others who belong to the covenant community.

The origins of a lectionary (in the sense of a set of public readings of God's word) and of preaching are often traced to the interesting account in Nehemiah 8. The whole passage reminds us what worship was and is. People gathered together (the basic meaning of the term 'synagogue') in a public place (verse 1) and everyone reverently and attentively listened as Ezra, the priest, read from 'the book of the law' (verses 3-5). All the way through the seven-day festival (in this case, of Tabernacles commemorating the long period following the exodus from Egypt when the people of Israel had only tents to live in as they travelled north towards Canaan), the law was read (verse 18). The most fascinating words so far as preaching is concerned, however, come in verse 8. Whilst the people stayed in their places, the Levites (verse 7): '. . . read from the book, from the law of God, with interpretation. They gave the sense, so that the people understood the reading.' This seems to indicate not mere translation but also commenting on the reading, that is, what we might call the meaning and application of the text.

Some 150 years earlier, King Josiah was presented with 'the book of the law' (thought to correspond to what we now have in Deuteronomy 12-26) after it had been stumbled across, presumably after neglect, during repairs to the Temple. The mere reading out loud to the elders, 'all the inhabitants of Jerusalem, the priests, the prophets, and all the people, both small and great' of this 'book of the covenant' (2 Kings 23:2) is, according to the account, what inspired a major reform, clearing out all foreign influences from the Temple and centralising worship there by abolishing all other sanctuaries.

By Ezra's time, the power of reading 'the book' is amplified by the benefits of exposition. Though only the scribes, the priests and the Levites are said to gather specifically 'to study the words of the law' (Nehemiah 8:13), everyone hears the reading and is given 'the sense' of it (verse 8). Most significantly, this mental process has a practical outcome, in this case, the keeping of the festival of Tabernacles.

The purpose of all preaching is similarly practical. It is meant not only to affirm belief but, alongside this, to make a difference, even to transform behaviour. When someone says, 'I love you' it is hardly 'for information only'. Overhearing someone say it may be, but for the person addressed, the words do something.

The prophetic word is constantly presented as doing something (Isaiah 55:10-11) even to the point of making someone drop dead (Jeremiah 28:16-17)! Sometimes it performs simply by going out into the ether, as it were. Often it requires a response from the 'hearer'. Without the response, the prophetic word has not really been heard. The prophet Ezekiel is scathing of those who gather to 'hear' his message as a sort of entertainment. They are, he says, like those who assemble to hear the singer of love songs, someone with a beautiful voice and who plays an instrument well (33:32). They want to be entertained in that they hear what he says but 'will not do it'.

Presumably both Ezekiel and Isaiah – whose message is, as we have seen, deafening and blinding in the worst possible sense (and all the other 'unheeded' prophets – which, let's face it, seems to be most of them!) were not to blame for the apparent ineffectiveness of their preaching. Their job was to be receptive themselves to receiving God's word, and then to proclaim it.

So today's preacher is commissioned to acquire and then transmit the word of God. The word, whether read, sung or dramatised, has to be proclaimed. Then it has to be interpreted, in terms which give the real, human beings in front of the preacher a fighting chance of responding to it. Whether any behaviour which needs transforming in any individual or group in the congregation actually gets transformed is surely outside the power of the preacher. But the Old Testament law and the prophets need to be read and preached on if Christians are to tap into these rich and unique sources of biblical tradition.

Attempts are made in contemporary liturgy to ensure that both the 'law and the prophets' of Jesus' own scriptures are read. The Covenant service of the Methodist tradition is an excellent illustration. This service grew out of John Wesley's own emphasis on a covenant relationship between God and his people. In its latest form, in *The Methodist Worship Book* of 1999, it is explicitly stated that, before a reading from the epistles and then from the Gospel, there is a reading first from the Law and then from the Prophets (p. 284). From the law, the lection is either Exodus 24:3-11 or Deuteronomy 29:10-19 and in response to the words 'For the wisdom that guides us', the people say: 'we praise you, O God.' The same response follows 'For the word that inspires us', after the prophetic reading of Jeremiah 31:31-34.

The question reappears: are we, the church, the people addressed by God in the Old Testament? We must decide. If not, then let us follow the logic of this through to its conclusion and drop any claim to being the people of God. If we dare to affirm the covenant, taking to ourselves the words: 'in order that he may establish you today as his people, and that he may be your God, as he promised you . . .' (Deuteronomy 29:13), then we must also follow the logic of this through to its conclusion and explore and identify with the promises and obligations which this covenant entails. This the latest version of the Methodist Covenant Service tries to do. So, for example, following the readings and the sermon (how could it neglect the Old Testament after all this?), comes a beautifully-worded section about God's making a covenant with the people Israel, renewing this covenant in Jesus Christ and in our present meeting 'to renew the covenant which bound them and binds us to God' (p. 285).

Repeatedly, in what is usually designated the holiness code (Leviticus 17-26) comes the succinct summary and motive for a covenant people: 'You shall be holy, for I the LORD your God am holy' (eg 19:2). The importance of holiness is, of course, not confined to the book of Leviticus. In Isaiah 6, the word 'holy' occurs in verse 3 (what has become the *trisagion* of Jewish and later also of Christian liturgy) and verse 13 and it is implied in verses 5 and 6, in the contrasting impurity of the prophet and his people and in the seraphs' cauterising action, respectively. The title 'Holy One of Israel' is a notable feature throughout the whole of the book of Isaiah. We find it also in Hosea (eg 11:9, 12).

We see in this concept the same sort of emphasis on relationship as we saw in the chapter 'Beginning with God'. Right through the Old Testament, if the beginning is always located in God, then the end is found in the human response. The roots of human conduct are seen to lie in relationship. As in the New Testament, God's undeserved love is presented as both the motive and pattern for action. Not loving your neighbour, in the ways spelt out in Leviticus and elsewhere in the Old Testament, is seen not merely as failure to observe an impersonal code but as disloyalty to God. To 'know' God, in the Old Testament, connotes both a knowledge of his requirements and a relationship with him which gives the impetus for fulfilling them (Hosea 2:19-20; Jeremiah 22:16). Hosea, on God's behalf, scornfully rejects Israel's cry: 'My God, we – Israel – know you!' because 'they have broken my covenant, and transgressed my law' (Hosea 8:1-2). For Hosea, the lack of knowledge of God is the fundamental problem with the people of Israel and their leaders (eg 4:1-6). 'Not my people' is a brutally clear name for him to give to one of his children, and it clearly reverses the covenant formula (1:8-9).

Whilst most Christians identify themselves with the covenant and its obligations in the sacrament of Holy Communion, the Salvation Army, with no sacraments, affirms the centrality of holiness differently. Its founder, William Booth, speaks of it as 'a fundamental truth', standing at 'the forefront of all our doctrines'. Every Sunday, the morning service takes the form of a 'holiness meeting' where the emphasis is on biblical exposition with the aim of 'sanctifying' the people. This is because 'all holiness has its source in the holiness of God'.[1]

Whatever our tradition, it is clear that we must avoid the false contrast of law and grace. We can and must preach the Old Testament law, drawing on the riches of the books of Exodus, Leviticus and Deuteronomy. In this law, or better *torah*, meaning direction, we find not just principles but also consequences and motives. We are clearly not espousing specific obligations such as the food laws in which meat and milk dishes are to be separated, as based on interpretation of Deuteronomy 14:21, for example, but we are taking for ourselves the whole legal tradition of the scriptures as the proclamation from a saving God to a saved people, acting out of gratitude. It is still up to us to work out the application of laws in our own, very different, situations. But we surely do need to call on the concrete application of the past in determining God's direction for the present. A good example of this comes in Deuteronomy 15 where the idea of a year for cancelling a neighbour's debts has provided both content and motive for Jubilee 2000 for many Christians.

'For you are a people holy to the LORD your God' (14:21) is not an optional extra for those who happen to 'like' the Old Testament. It is both a proclamation and a working definition for those who want to be the people of God. In coming to a conclusion in reply to the recurrent question in this chapter: are you 'this people'(?), it may be useful to recognise that its source, Isaiah 6:9-10, is quoted in all four gospels with reference to people's rejection of Jesus' message (Matthew 13:14-15; Mark 4:12; Luke 8:10; John 12:37-43). Luke also quotes it at the end of Acts of the Apostles (28:26-27). Though it is there applied to Jewish leaders forfeiting, in Paul's view, their claim to be God's people to Gentiles because 'they will listen' (verse 28), it may be salutary for members of any tradition, at any time, to remember that there is nothing automatic about either becoming or staying the people of God.

Further Reading

R E Clements, *Deuteronomy*, JSOT Press, Sheffield 1989.
Lester L Grabbe, *Leviticus*, JSOT Press, Sheffield 1993.
W Johnstone, *Exodus*, JSOT Press, Sheffield 1990.
H M G Williamson, *Ezra and Nehemiah*, JSOT Press, Sheffield 1987.

7

TELLING THE TRUTH

One of the questions most frequently asked of the Old Testament is: 'Is it true?' The question may be asked of descriptions of creation which science may seem to contradict. In a survey of religious belief early in 2000, one of the questions asked was whether Christians believed in the literal truth of creation in six days. It is a pity that they were not asked whether they believed in a creator God – no matter what the time-scale and no matter whether the order corresponded to the account in Genesis 1:1-2:4a or to that in Genesis 2:4b-24. It has always puzzled me why both the literalists and those who taunt them are not troubled by the question of whether Genesis says human beings were created first or last. What does it mean to ask: 'Is it true?' It may be asked of accounts of events which are inexplicable except in terms of a God who intervenes to overcome powerful enemies or even nature itself in order to save his people. It may also be asked of material containing laws which we somehow cannot comprehend God giving to anyone, and certainly not to us.

At the first whiff of the suggestion that something recorded in the Old Testament did not really happen Christians may get upset. This applies even more so to events and sayings recorded in the New Testament, especially in the gospels. The media seems to have a positive obsession with this threat to belief as they see it. I recall, for instance, hearing George Carey preach in Canterbury Cathedral one Easter Sunday. When I saw the television news coverage later that day, I was astonished to hear that he had denied the resurrection of Jesus. In fact, he did no such thing. Nor was there scope for anyone really listening to the sermon to confuse the Archbishop with the former Bishop of Durham, David Jenkins, who delighted the same obsessive media by once suggesting that some people view the resurrection as 'a conjuring trick with bones'. The feeling that misguided Christians will sooner or later have to concede that the Bible is not true quite often surfaces in those sceptical or even scoffing of all religious faith. More worrying is the anxiety which this can encourage among Christians themselves that they might indeed be being taken for a ride.

One response to this has been for Christians to attempt to shore up the truth of the Bible by finding explanations which make the accounts more acceptable to the sceptics. In the book of Joshua, the walls of Jericho come tumbling down because of marching feet or, rather more convincingly, an earthquake. In the book of Exodus, the pillar of cloud is really a tornado and the pillar of fire a volcano. The sea 'parts' because of a particular type of reedbed or wind. (We may compare the suggestions of squalls and sandbanks offered to get rid of the suggestion in the gospels, thought preposterous by the sceptics, that Jesus stilled the storm or walked on the water.) Besides needing more believing than the original stories, these suggestions leave one wondering: 'So what?' Just what would we have established if it could be confirmed once and for all that Jericho's walls collapsed either because of vigorous human activity, natural causes or superhuman intervention?

Further unwarranted excitement sometimes arises from archaeological discoveries which are considered to 'prove' the authenticity of the biblical record. Whatever archaeology can establish about the existence of the city of Jericho at a particular time, it can hardly demonstrate that a destruction was carried out by Joshua and his men. The Bible claims that it was. Furthermore, it claims that this was a manifestation of God who responded to his people's obedience by enabling them to conquer this and other cities in the 'promised land'.

As we approach many of the Old Testament books with a view to preaching, it is this second aspect of the biblical claim about the fall of Jericho which perhaps gives us a clue. We need to get beyond the question of literal truth in relation to these books, not because we are suddenly losing our nerve in the face of persistent challenge and contradiction, but because the books themselves get beyond the question of literal truth. 'Did the snake really speak?' would hardly be the most vital question to ask the writer of Genesis 3 should we meet him (and I am not convinced that we should add 'or her'). Even a carefully-prepared chat-show host would not insult the writer of Exodus 3 by asking: 'What sort of bush was it and how did it just go on burning?' That 'truth is stranger than fiction' and that 'the facts are sacred' are both claims worthy of investigation when it comes to the Old Testament and how to preach on it.

Attention will be focused first of all on examples from the so-called historical books of the Old Testament and then on examples more naturally described as story than history. (Sometimes the two are intermingled as, for example, in the cycles of stories about Elijah and Elisha in 1 and 2 Kings.) The terms 'saga', 'legend' and 'myth' are deliberately being avoided here as our immediate concern is not to attempt a detailed consideration of literary genres, for which many books are required and do exist. It is rather to reclaim in some way sections of the Old Testament often neglected by those seriously interested in theology and sometimes misused, as indicated above, by those who for some peculiar reason lose their everyday awareness of the varieties of 'truth' when it comes to biblical narrative.

The books of Joshua, Judges, Samuel and Kings are referred to by Old Testament scholars as the Deuteronomistic history. This term signifies that these books, as we now have them, owe their existence to writers belonging to the Deuteronomistic school of thought. What this school wrote, or at least edited, was no dispassionate account of historical events. Rather its members were religious historians composing, from the perspective of the Babylonian exile of the sixth century BC, an interpretation of Israel's experience. At the heart of this interpretation, and at the heart of the book of Deuteronomy, as we saw in the chapter 'Being the people of God', were the convictions that God was one and required purity of worship, that God had elected the people Israel and entered into a covenant with them, and that he had given them a land in which they were to practise obedience to this covenant. The reign of each king is, therefore, judged according to that king's capacity to maintain this obedience. By this criterion, for example, the ninth century King Ahab is condemned (1 Kings 16:29-34) because he failed to avoid the temptation to worship other gods (1 Kings 17-18) and did not uphold the moral and religious demands of regarding land as God's gift and of fair and honest legal dealings (1 Kings 21). His father, Omri, for all that he is known from Assyrian and Moabite records to have made Israel militarily, politically and geographically strong, is dismissed in a verse because 'he did what was evil in the sight of the LORD' (1 Kings 16:25).

The facts which the Deuteronomistic historian presents are indeed sacred, not in the sense of giving us accurate information (non-Israelite records are in that sense more accurate about Omri, for instance), but in the sense of taking events as Israel experienced them and ascribing to them a sacred significance. Though the days of biblical scholarship are gone when everything in the Old Testament was pushed into the mode of 'salvation history' as the only important factor, nonetheless, these 'histories' are offered, both to those who first read them and to Christian congregations regarding themselves as belonging to the present people of God, as the truth. This truth is indeed stranger than fiction. Whatever elements, both of what we would call strictly fiction and strictly non-fiction, go into the rich mix of the Deuteronomistic histories, the truth they claim is often strange, especially to our modern ears. It may, moreover, be challenged. So, for instance, Michael Prior urges us to reject any suggestion that God's giving the people of Israel the land means that it is morally right that they should exterminate the indigenous people.[1] In terms of modern application, a question about the theological basis of land ownership is surely far more vital than what physically happened at Jericho.

The narrators of the Joshua stories to some extent agree that what they are after is meaning. So, they maintain, were the Israelites themselves in search of meaning. We read in 4:21-24 that Joshua instructs the Israelites when their children ask them about twelve stones taken out of the River Jordan: 'What do these stones mean?' to respond: 'Israel crossed over the Jordan here on dry ground.' Thus they link their history with that of their ancestors escaping from Egypt and this, says the writer, 'so that all the people of the earth may know that the hand of the LORD is mighty, and so that you may fear the LORD your God forever.' Whilst Michael Prior would hardly see eye to eye with the writer either of certain Joshua or certain Exodus narratives, he is concerned, as were the writers, with truth at a far deeper level than the literal. They are both asking what the real agenda is in the Old Testament. And so must any Christian preacher.

The preacher should ask, as did many Old Testament writers, why, in view of this 'conquest' should the Israelites have lost the land? A Christian Zionism which simply whisks out of the Old Testament God's promises of 'the land' whilst ignoring God's demands for justice (which in the Old Testament always means far more even than fairness) for the vulnerable is surely a highly dangerous thing. A corrective to this in recent years have been the Liberation theological readings of many of the biblical narratives, as represented by Prior.

These are permeating 'popular' readings of the Old Testament, as evidenced by the Radio 4 broadcast of John McCarthy's *Bible Journey*.[2] Starting with Moses, he went, via Jesus' 'Blessed are the poor', to El Salvador and the martyrdom in 1980 of Archbishop Romero. John McCarthy showed, in interviews ranging from modern Christians in El Salvador to the sceptic Tony Benn, who engagingly revealed that he 'had always seen Marx as the last of the Old Testament prophets', that the Exodus narratives are about being set free and the commandments are about the conditions for a peaceful society. Coming from McCarthy, formerly himself in captivity for over five years and from Christians working for peace in El Salvador, it was powerful to hear at the close of the broadcast the claim that people put the Bible to use to help them understand their circumstances and to cope with them, to give them dignity and hope.

The Old Testament itself, especially in the historical books, raises questions which are of immense, even urgent, importance for human conduct – personal, national and international. What norms does God work to according to these books and are these theological narratives valid? But the unconvinced may still ask why we should attend to such questions. After all, it is not immediately obvious what Joshua and Omri have to do with my history. Why not study the history of the Chinese? It is hardly that the figures of the Old Testament are held up as people to emulate. Moral examples many of them are not. Why, in 1999, did I go, like so many 'pilgrims', all the way to the site of the ancient Beersheba? I was not expecting to see incontrovertible evidence of the well where Abraham settled a water dispute (Genesis 21:27-32) nor on the most ancient of stones some indication that Beersheba once marked the southern border of the land (eg Judges 20:1), nor that Elijah fled there escaping from Queen Jezebel (1 Kings 19:3). Impressive as the site was, it did not 'prove' the Old Testament, nor was the despondent Elijah a very good role model. But the archaeological excavations there do confirm its role as a religious centre. Its worship was criticised by Amos (5:5; 8:14) and it seems to have been among the sanctuaries targeted in the reform of King Josiah (2 Kings 23:8). Moreover they establish that the city, complete with fortifications, private dwellings, a governor's palace and a well, was founded in the twelfth or eleventh century BC.

Christian pilgrims go to Beersheba because they link their history with these ancient times and because they link their history with the biblical characters of these ancient times. It would not be sensible to suggest that they concern themselves instead with the history of the Chinese. The New Testament presents Jesus' God as the God of Israel, and the Old Testament presents the God of Israel as not only the God of the whole earth but a God peculiarly active in the response, unpromising though this often was, of the people of that ancient land. It may not be immediately obvious to me that Ahab and Jezebel have influenced my spiritual history but, somehow, the preacher has to make it obvious.

This will surely not be achieved by dragging me through literary and historical difficulties in narratives about the patriarchs. But it may be achieved by an exploration of what the narratives themselves seem to want to convey about these three men – and, some would add, the matriarchs. It will not do much for my faith or practice to debate the site of the crossing of the sea, but if the preacher neglects the enormous impact of the exodus event on Old Testament, and consequently on New Testament, imagery, there will be an enormous hole in my grasp of what it might mean to belong to the people of God, whether in the past or in the present.

If telling the truth is the key criterion, what part may telling the story play? What is the connection, if any, between telling the story and telling the truth? For anything like the spread of the Old Testament to be represented, preaching must include a different sort of narrative from that so far considered. Whilst history is non-fiction, even if interpreted, within many Old Testament books there is also fiction or story, in some cases constituting the whole of an Old Testament book. Again, it is easy to become deflected and ask questions which, whilst they may be quite interesting, are not at all important to the Old Testament writers.

A few years ago, the figure of Jonah was taken as a sort of 'theme' for a local arts festival. As part of this, a new opera was performed by hundreds of schoolchildren in Canterbury Cathedral. So far as I know, nobody in the audience got upset at the thought that the whale was not represented in the way in which they might, from the biblical story, have imagined it and no one left with the burning question: 'When did all this first happen?' How much less will a modern congregation need a definitive answer to questions about whales or just what happened when. The historical period of the story's composition may well be significant, but only secondarily so far as preaching is concerned. It may help establish the message of the book or part of the book. To get stuck on the question: 'Did Jonah exist?' is about as pointless as asking whether the characters in Jesus' parables existed. If someone gave me indisputable proof that there never was a man who found treasure buried in a field in Palestine who then went and sold all that he had and bought this field (Matthew 13:44) nor a man called Jonah who tried to escape preaching repentance to the people of Nineveh, would it matter?

The Old Testament has some ripping good yarns to offer, if nothing else. They are full of surprises and, as the *News of the World* would put it, 'all human life is there' – and not only the human. A particularly stimulating rediscovering of 'the brilliance and power' of many of the stories in the book of Genesis as well as, so the cover puts it, 'their significance for the contemporary Church' is to be found in Trevor Dennis' *Looking God in the Eye*.[3] He stresses, for instance, the intimacy of the God the sound of whose footsteps is heard in the garden (Genesis 3:8) and the human response to this intimacy, with Adam and later Cain eventually learning to face God and speak with him.[4] Abraham, on the other hand, has no difficulty in speaking up. In a chapter headed 'Telling God how to be God', Dennis explores Genesis 18:16-33, in which Abraham gives God a lesson in justice over the people of Sodom. Like the Rabbis in their 'commentaries' (*midrashim*) on such stories, Dennis encourages the imagination. He does not try to calm everything down, iron it out, or all the other sanitising things preachers are sometimes guilty of when trying to make the God of the Old Testament acceptable or at least predictable. Mechanical views of justice are in Genesis 18, as in the book of Jonah, turned upside down. Nor can apparent contradictions always be dealt with. How, for instance, does some of this square with the merciful yet relentlessly just God of Exodus 34:6-7? Dennis does not here deal with Genesis 22 and the story of 'the binding of Isaac', but many Old Testament scholars with an interest in preaching do.[5]

It may even be that sometimes we simply read or tell the story, or part of it, and leave it at that. If this be objected to on the ground that it is not preaching on the Old Testament, then neither, I would contend, is wrecking the story by taming the chief character, God. The Old Testament stories can take this, if it is done well. I once attended a workshop for preachers conducted by 'Storytellers', the Bible Society's 'Open Book' project in partnership with The Northumbria Community. Each of us was taught to tell from memory a small part of the story of Elijah and the widow of Zarephath (1 Kings 17:8-16). The text was the NRSV but we had to memorise it and then tell it as a story, rather than reciting it parrot-fashion. We all surprised ourselves by our capacity to acquire this skill in the limited time available, at least with the one or two verses allocated to each of us. It was definitely not acting, but storytelling.

We also had a demonstration of the telling in such a way of the story of Shadrach, Meshach and Abednego in King Nebuchadnezzar's fiery furnace (Daniel 3). This was done, with enormous power, by a member of the Storytellers' team. It had taken him days to learn this and, we were told, it was still getting better each time he told it. Though each preacher may not regularly have the time for such 'acquiring' of a story for telling in worship, one or more members of the congregation might have, or the preacher, occasionally and over a long period of time, might manage it. Whether we make the effort depends on how much value we attach to these stories – whether as communication in themselves or as the basis for an actual sermon.

We must be careful if we do say anything about the story, rather than just reading/telling it, that we are not simply giving information, especially if it is identical information to that contained in the story, only given less well. We are, after all, presenting the Old Testament story within the context of worship. There, people are wanting to find meaning, often but not always, of course, best conveyed by story. They are wanting to be inspired to worship. Whether or not a conventional sermon is involved, the preacher must, in this context, ask of the treatment of the story: 'What am I intending to convey and to what purpose?' Whether history or story, the congregation needs to know what 'the big idea' is, just as surely as with other types of Old Testament material.

We should be sure, as preachers, when we choose our story and decide how it is going to be heard, that we know how it might challenge, disturb or comfort. What, in the rest of our worship, are we going to do about its impact? What impact do we hope it will have on next week's living for the people of God, as constituted before us? If there is not at some point emerging from the story, or from the silence, the prayers, the music or the songs which follow it, some witness to the reality of a God to whom people feel able to respond, why tell it? It is good practice in Religious Education in schools always to ask what you want to convey by telling a Bible story. What are children supposed to do with impressions left from the story of the flood, for instance? And do not be fooled that all they care about are the animals going in 'two by two'. What comfort is this when so much life is wiped out by this God who does not seem to know how to handle what he has made?

This is not to be construed as a plea to reduce the story to a message. For there is so much more than 'a message' to the Old Testament stories, with their rhythms and repetitions, their orderliness, and their surprising gaps in the narrative, where the writers are simply not interested in what happened next in the sense of giving the whole story for future play-acting. In, for example, Amos 7:10-17 we never are told how Jeroboam, the king, responds to the complaint of Amaziah, the priest, about Amos, the prophet. Attempts have been made to reconstruct the exact order of events in Hosea's love life (based on Hosea 1 and 3 and possibly 2), but if it was so vital that we needed to know this in order to get any worthwhile message from this prophetic book, would not the writer and/or editor have made a better job of it? The clues to what matters come very often in the biblical text itself. Worrying about whether there is such an historical figure as Adam, Abraham, Jonah, Hosea or even Moses is not the right issue for the preacher. At issue is trying to make sense of the notion that God acts in human history and that he requires a response from a community of faith. 'Is this true?' is what we should ask.

The compilers of the belief-survey of 2000 would probably not even begin to understand the question. Nor would the reporters hanging around our cathedrals waiting for eminent clerics to trip themselves up and deny something vital about the faith. But the preacher should beware sinking simply into religious jargon. When tempted to be smug, the preacher should ask how, if questioned, he or she would defend such assertions that God does act in the history of a people. How is it true? Telling the truth is, in preaching, never far away from finding meaning. The Old Testament, in its reading and exposition, provides us with unique stories which afford us unique ways of telling the truth.

Further Reading

Adrian H W Curtis, *Joshua*, JSOT Press, Sheffield 1994.
P R Davies, *Daniel*, JSOT Press, Sheffield 1985.
Jonathan Magonet, *Bible Lives*, SCM Press, London 1992.
J W Rogerson, *Genesis 1-11*, JSOT Press, Sheffield 1991.
R B Salters, *Jonah and Lamentations*, JSOT Press, Sheffield 1994.

8

MAKING SENSE OF EXPERIENCE

If there is one expectation of the sermon, it is that it will help the listeners make sense of experience. This is a tall order. Some people may, moreover, think the expectation totally unrealistic, because they have already come to the conclusion that experience does not make much, if any, sense. This view is itself represented in the Old Testament in a variety of ways. One manifestation is the cry of bewilderment and even despair. We see such cries in the prophetic literature in the book of Jeremiah (eg 15:18). The main occurrence of these protests against the apparent nonsense of experience is, however, in what is sometimes called the wisdom literature.

Under the heading of 'wisdom' come the biblical books of Job, Proverbs and Ecclesiastes. There are also certain psalms whose style and content classifies them as wisdom, eg Psalms 1; 37; 49. Scholars vary in the number of psalms which they feel fall into this category, but all are agreed on these three. Traditionally the category of Old Testament wisdom included also the whole book of Psalms and the Song of Songs. Though all classified as wisdom, these books do not all belong to one literary genre. Rather, as is now recognised, there is a wide range of different genres within these traditional 'wisdom' books, some best described as lament, some as disputation, some as hymn, and some as narrative prose.

Our attention will be directed firstly to the wisdom psalms and then to some psalms of lament, resurrecting from chapter 5 our interest in what sort of sentiments about God are appropriately voiced in worship. Job's protests against God will then be considered particularly against the backdrop of the religious believer's trying to make sense of experience. Next the way in which the book of Ecclesiastes tackles the apparent nonsense of it all will be related to the preacher's task. Finally, some attempt will be made to assess the book of Proverbs as a basis for Christian preaching.

Preachers are sometimes accused of answering the questions that no one is asking. This perception reflects the kind of sermon which, perhaps by attempting to be original, grows rather desperate and so ignores both exegesis of the text and attention to people's experiences. Much of the wisdom literature of the Old Testament springs out of questions and, by contrast with the desperate sermon, these are the ones which people are asking.

The 'wise' or the 'sages' who lie behind these texts are those who have pondered life's experiences and come up with some conclusion, which they pass on to those prepared to learn from them, their disciples. The writer of Psalm 37, it may be claimed, retains serious misgivings about whether reality corresponds to his faith. This claim about the psalmist is made on the ground that he 'doth protest too much'. He specifically urges people, at least three times, not to 'fret' at the apparent good time being had by the 'wicked' (verses 1,7,8). Moreover, every single one of this psalm's 40 verses is concerned to recommend joining the 'righteous' because, come what may, and despite temporary circumstances which may indicate otherwise, God 'rescues them from the wicked, and saves them, because they take refuge in him' (verse 40). A question which immediately arises for the would-be faithful of today regards the definition of 'righteousness' or, as other texts put it, 'wisdom'. 'The fear of the LORD is the beginning of wisdom' says the author of Psalm 111:10, and today's preacher could well explore this text, examining what the words either side of the 'is' actually amount to in terms of the psalmist's experience and ours. It is worth noting that

Psalm 49 indicates that this life alone is insufficient for the full working out of God's vindication (verse 15). The same is true of another Psalm often regarded as a wisdom psalm, namely, Psalm 73 (verse 24).

A major question, asked no less now than in Old Testament times, is 'Why does the way of the wicked prosper?' Admittedly, it is not put in these terms. Rather it usually appears in the form of 'Why do good people suffer?' or 'What has such a good person done to deserve this?' Whichever way it is formulated, the question concerns rewards. It rests on a prior assumption that God is just. Hence, the challenge to God which accompanies so many of these outcries, as in Jeremiah's 'You will be in the right, O LORD, when I lay charges against you: but let me put my case to you . . .' (12:1). Jeremiah's protest includes the related question of how long this unjust state of affairs will continue (verse 4). It is, we may conclude, inevitable that Jeremiah receives not an answer, but a challenge, indicating that things are going to get an awful lot worse. Nor is there even the additional assurance: '. . . before they get better' (verse 5).

What is vitally important for the Christian preacher, however, is that the question is asked. The New Testament, like so much of the Old, seems to present the view that people receive their just desert. Admittedly, this is often pushed into the future in the form of being on God's right hand in everlasting bliss – or on God's left in everlasting torment. Meanwhile clear-cut divisions, by fellow human beings at least, are rather dangerous, risking ripping up the wheat with the tares. Nonetheless, the good and the godly are 'like trees planted by streams of water . . . In all that they do, they prosper' (Psalm 1:3). This fundamental trust in the fairness of God, and of life's operation in his world, permeates the book of Deuteronomy and the Deuteronomistic histories, as seen in chapter 7. Consequently, good kings, by which is meant kings who are faithful to the God of Israel, notably, and almost exclusively, Josiah (2 Kings 22-23 and Jeremiah 22:15,16) flourish. Conversely, bad kings come to a sticky end.

This view is challenged in the psalm of lament. There are two types, the communal and the individual lament. The former invoke God's help in time of national catastrophe, recall his help in the past, and normally express confidence in his future answer. Protest rather than passive acceptance of suffering is a characteristic feature (eg Psalm 80). The individual lament is the largest single category in the psalter. Psalm 13 is typical. Its anguished cry of 'How long?' occurs four times in the first two verses. Then there is appeal to God (verse 3) followed by a joyful anticipation of an answer from God in the form of a reversal of the psalmist's present plight.

It is a very interesting exercise to go through a major denominational hymnbook to see how many psalms of lament are represented, whether in the form of paraphrase, metrical psalm or hymns which make significant allusions to psalms, or in the form of being printed for congregational use as, for example, a selection of over 50 in *Hymns & Psalms*.[1] In this particular example, it is striking how very little genuine doubt or protest is allowed to appear. Remembering the number of laments in the Old Testament makes me wonder, as in chapter 5, whether this is an advantage or a disadvantage to our worship. If not said or sung, should not these psalms at least sometimes be preached on?

It would seem that to the psalmist some experiences simply cannot be made sense of. Suffering seems to be a 'normal' part of life. Where is the equivalent of Psalm 13 in *Hymns & Psalms*? By contrast members of the Iona Community have been brave enough (or foolish enough, depending on your viewpoint) in one of their hymnbooks simply to include the psalmist's appeal to God to rescue them. In other hymns/songs/psalms they will affirm that this is precisely what he does, but here they have not included the assurance (Psalm 13:5,6) so common in psalms of lament (eg Psalm 22:21b-31). This could well be a useful corrective to the Christian tendency to stress that what matters in these psalms is actually the final confidence. There are psalms of confidence (eg 121 and, of course, 23) but we should not be quick to get to the 'happy ending'. As has often been remarked, Jesus was not, in his use of Psalm 22 (Matthew 27:46).

'Sometimes we have to call on God's care because we have been made redundant, victimised, lost out in love or been hurt by people close to us. At such times the words of Psalm 13 can be very helpful.' So read the words after the setting of Psalm 13 by the Iona Community, 'How long, O Lord?'[2] The directions given are 'slow and bluesy'! A sort of 'King David sings the blues' could perhaps fall flat on its face in worship, but, with the high quality of composition which comes from this Community, it works – given, of course, the right atmosphere and occasion.

It has been said that there is no genuine doubt in the Old Testament, not in the modern sense of doubting God's existence.[3] This would seem to be true of the psalms where only the fool denies him altogether (Psalm 14:1). The psalmist, on the other hand, finds God real enough to be argued with and thinks that he is worth arguing with. This is in itself a tremendous assertion of faith. Perhaps this is the clue to the inclusion of the psalm of lament in the hymnbook of ancient Israel. If it is largely absent from our hymnbooks, the explanation must somehow lie with us.

Not everyone agrees that the key question of the book of Job is similarly: 'Why do good people suffer?' Alternative suggestions include: 'How can people obtain what might be called a working knowledge of God?' and 'Is there such a thing as disinterested faith or disinterested goodness?' It is often remarked that in God's thundering replies to Job's complaints, no answer is given, certainly not as to why he is suffering so terribly. Perhaps we are wrong to seek a central theme in the book. Certainly in preaching we are not obliged to have each theory sorted, all possibilities covered and weighed as if we were producing a convincing academic lecture or article.

Nonetheless, it is hard to escape the conviction that somehow in the book of Job God himself is in the dock and this because his dealings with the world do not correspond to what people might expect. The age-old problem of theodicy does seem to loom quite large. In other words, how can the reality of evil, here experienced in the form of suffering – undeserved in Job's view and somehow deserved in the view of his counsellors – be squared with the existence of a God who is both all-powerful and all-good? As the dilemma runs, if he is all-powerful, he must surely be able to prevent or eliminate evil. If he is all-good, he must surely want to. Yet somehow evil remains. What then can we preach from Job?

Whatever it is, it must surely have something to do with the human need, if not for complete explanation of our experience, at least for some clue to keep us going. It is often suggested that the main contribution of the book is its apparent rebellion against the received wisdom. More convincing is the notion that it represents one facet common to the wisdom tradition, namely, wrestling with the contradictions of life. Through the drama, the preacher may be drawn into the way in which, not through neat answers, but rather through struggling with these remaining contradictions, some disclosure of God is given and ultimately some peace found in a real relationship with God.

Many years ago, the Old Testament scholar, H Wheeler Robinson wrote an influential book suggesting that God himself suffering alongside his creation was a concept much in evidence in the Old Testament, long before it played such a major role in the New Testament.[4] But before we quickly Christianise the book of Job and offer it as a forerunner of the redemptive suffering of Jesus, perhaps we should note the universal concerns of this book. Like much other wisdom literature of the Old Testament, it is non-national in its character. The stress is not on Israel as a community, but on individuals wrestling with the frustrations, even agonies, of experience. This is the strength of this literature and it somehow lies at the heart of what can valuably be preached.

Although it is dangerous to suggest that the various wisdom books are all saying the same thing, there are certain characteristics of what is recommended for 'the good life'. These include attentiveness to God, sometimes in silence, and a humility in recognising that our best intellectual efforts do not stop life from being enigmatic, sometimes painfully so. There is also an understanding that we cannot always shape our experience, that, in the context of God's eternity, an acceptance of the timeliness of a whole range of experiences, positive and negative, may be the only option, and an honesty which refuses the comfort of explanations which do not ring true. All these fall within the orbit of the spiritual experience of human beings. As we have seen in many other types of literature in the Old Testament, knowledge of God and the way in which this may be acquired, whether through prayer and contemplation or through priestly and prophetic teaching and obeying the torah, becomes a constant goal.

Another struggle to make sense of experience which rather looks as if it has given up on the challenge concludes: 'All is vanity.' That these are words uttered by no less than Koheleth, usually rendered 'the preacher' of Ecclesiastes (3:19; 12:8) may seem rather discouraging. As of all the other Old Testament books, we may profitably ask the traditio-historical questions about this book, including: when was it written, how was it written, and why was it written? Such questions always have a bearing on the interpretation of the book. The preacher in his or her preparation may go into these questions with varying degrees of detail. The discoveries may also be shared in part with the subsequent congregation. But the person to whom this book is addressed is primarily a preacher and not a teacher. What is sometimes given as 'background', an off-putting introduction if ever there was one, is not in itself preaching and, unless its consequences have been truly integrated into the sermon, it would be better not mentioned. One aspect of Ecclesiastes which does have a bearing on how its contents are preached is that it contains many quotations, which would be recognisable to its readers, even if not acknowledged (eg 1:15; 1:18). Sometimes contradictory quotations are offered and it would seem that the writer is deliberately drawing attention to the fact that reality does not admit of clear descriptions or even clear recommendations.

The author of Ecclesiastes is essentially a sceptic, in the sense that he refuses to accept as given what might be expected of the pious. As we have seen, he is in good company with many in the Old Testament who feel that fear of God and wisdom do not consist in swallowing platitudes or half-truths. They involve doubting God, even railing against him, not because he might not exist but precisely because, since he does exist, he has a lot to answer for, so far as people experience life's reality.

What Koheleth questions is the human experience of suffering and particularly unjust suffering, in that the sufferers cannot in any way be said to have brought it upon themselves. Perhaps, then, this chapter would be better headed 'interpreting experience'. Essentially that is what not only the preacher and his hearers are trying to do, but also what the characters, thinkers and writers of the Old Testament itself were trying to do. But neither they nor we start from the neutral position that experience may or may not make sense. They believed in a certain sort of God, a God who was loving, just, and powerful to save. It was when experience to all intents and purposes belied this belief that their desperate cries were uttered.

The inevitability of death is particularly emphasised in Ecclesiastes (eg 2:13-16; 3:20;12:7). In various ways, it makes a mockery of life, especially of human pretensions. Nonetheless, the good life is presented as the satisfying life, in so far as it seeks to be illuminated by God's wisdom. 'The preacher', usually judged to be particularly gloomy, in fact sounds positively cheerful compared with Job shouting and the Psalmist weeping!

Many of us, whether preachers or preached to, are nervous of the approach which refers us to biblical responses to solve our particular conundrum. The list in the front of a Gideons' Bible may offer us a suggested passage to read when variously perplexed, anxious or in despair. It has become something of a cliché to say that there are no easy answers. When a preacher ends this way, we may be tempted to ask why he or she has dragged us through the various possible answers if they are so unsatisfactory. When trying to make sense of experience, as with every sermon, the preacher must establish precisely what it is he or she wants to convey, and to what effect. Simply leaving everything up in the air is hardly likely to constitute a worthwhile experience for a congregation.

High in the charts in 1979 there was a very catchy number by Ian Dury and the Blockheads entitled, 'Reasons to be cheerful: part three'. In these words prefacing lists of items of experience which may or may not add a little zest to life, this rap-style song rather sent up the 'count your blessings' response to feeling down. Is the book of Proverbs an early version of this response to experience? The book is, after all, an alarmingly optimistic collection. And if it is, can we preach on it? How also can we avoid becoming moralistic, even banal? Perhaps one method is to use the occasional proverb as a pointer or reminder of some of the major Old Testament emphases on God's justice and providence and to assert the desperately needed belief that somehow the way we behave affects the total of human goodness in a world based on his laws. What many proverbs are presenting, after all, is the attractiveness of the person of faith who genuinely takes delight in trying to follow God's will. Perhaps Psalm 1 is not so far removed from reality after all, nor so far removed from Psalms 37 and 49. Without wanting to make its message so innocuous that it is not worth uttering, perhaps it offers the preacher the chance to preach on virtue being its own reward in a way that does not conjure up the caricatured idealist or the maligned do-gooder.

The book of Proverbs may not, then, be unreasonably optimistic. Many of its sayings are not only earthy but also 'ring true'. This fact, in itself, makes them eminently preachable. Not every sermon need plumb profound theological depths. Sometimes the pithy, the simple, and the obvious may need stating and mulling over. Some of the Proverbs strike us as humorous (eg 22:13) and this because they correspond to human experience and what it has taught us. Old Testament wisdom, especially the book of Proverbs, may even have a special claim on our congregations, precisely because it distils the experience of everyone, not necessarily Israelite. When the Gideons first added to their New Testaments, as placed in hotel bedrooms, it was the book of Proverbs that they chose, along with the Psalms. It may be argued that this was because its theology was always anchored in universal, down-to-earth concerns.

We see this clearly in Proverbs 8 where the writer's characteristic emphasis on God's wisdom's existing before creation (verses 22-30) is combined with his equally characteristic emphasis that fundamentally wisdom is expressed in discretion, humility and honest speech (verses 12-13). These are attainable values and can be advocated. Their opposites can be condemned as a healthy corrective to our apparent obsession with sexual mores. Jesus and Paul have so much more to say about how we talk about other people than they do about sexual relations. This realism about the power of words, whether to help or to damage other people, is rooted in the Old Testament. It is not that the wisdom writers are blind to the harm done by adultery and jealousy (eg Proverbs 6:24,29,34; 7:5). Rather, they take in the wide sweep of life as experienced by just about everyone.

It may be fashionable to stick with Jeremiah, Job and the Psalmist 'at a bad moment' and say that life is grossly unfair and that we do right maybe to mention this to a God who is said, in the Old Testament, to excel in right dealings. At least, come clean and admit that there is a problem and do not give pat answers which do not fit life's realities.

Against this, a plea may be made for the reassurances of the other wisdom literature to be found in the Old Testament. If we cannot preach on the justice and righteousness of God any longer, then what can we preach on? What are we saying has happened since this literature was penned, or at least since the close of the Old Testament canon, which has altered reality? Some would maintain, whether personally, nationally or internationally, that something has happened which renders belief in God's justice incredible. The sudden and premature death of an only child, or a brutal civil war, or the Holocaust, for example, may deprive people of their faith in a God who is loving and powerful. People have, indeed, been so deprived. But does this alter the need to proclaim belief in such a God? If we take the view that the term 'God' refers to something more, or at least other, than a human construct, then we may just have to carry on preaching God's justice, in the face of all that mocks it.

Whether in snappy proverbs or skilfully crafted speeches, the wisdom literature offers a useful, even essential, balance to Christian preaching which thinks that all its concerns must be distinctively Christian in the sense of dealing always with the crucifixion rather than on how you get on with your neighbour or employer. Whether in fragments or extended argument, truth is presented in these Old Testament books in a way that is accessible to anyone who may just try listening to an Old Testament passage and a sermon dealing with it as a method of making sense of experience. Like so much else in the Old Testament, the books mentioned in this chapter may thus get the preacher a hearing with a method and a message which might otherwise be missed.

The much-talked of 'culture gap' between us and the Old Testament is a red herring. Is the gap really much greater than that between us and the New Testament? After all, my world is not characterised by lepers and Gerasene demoniacs any more than it is by sacrifices and foreign alliances – perhaps even less! 'It's life, Jim, but not as we know it' is some people's verdict on what we find in the Old Testament. It cannot be the preacher's verdict.

Further Reading

Robert Davidson, *Wisdom and Worship*, SCM Press, London 1990.
J H Eaton, *Job*, JSOT Press, Sheffield 1985.
J H Eaton, *The Contemplative Face of Old Testament Wisdom*, SCM Press, London 1989.
J D Martin, *Proverbs*, JSOT Press, Sheffield 1995.
R N Whybray, *Ecclesiastes*, JSOT Press, Sheffield 1989.

NOTES

Chapter 1

1 W Brueggemann, *Isaiah 40-66*, Westminster John Knox Press, Louisville 1998, p.122.

2 'Which Commentary shall I buy?', *Worship &Preaching*, October-December 1992, pp. 8-9.

Chapter 2

1 Excellent summaries of these approaches are offered in John H Hayes and Carl R Holladay, *Biblical Exegesis*, 2nd edition, SCM Press, London 1988, and John Rogerson [ed], *Beginning Old Testament Study*, 2nd edition, SPCK, London 1998. Fuller indication of their value for preaching is offered by David L Bartlett, *Between the Bible and the Church*, Abingdon Press, Nashville 1999.

2 In *Preaching to the Exiles*, Basil Blackwell, Oxford.

3 Examples of this can be found in David M Gunn and Danna Nolan Fewell, *Narrative and the Hebrew Bible*, Oxford University Press, Oxford 1993, pp. 90-100. The book also has provocative sections on Genesis 2-3;4; 38; Judges, Samuel and Jonah.

4 Phyllis Trible, *Texts of Terror*, SCM Press, London 1984, p.28.

5 P Barber [ed], 3rd edition revised, Methodist Publishing House, Peterborough 1999, p. 30.

Chapter 3

1 Methodist Publishing House, Peterborough 1999, p. 331.

2 Elizabeth Achtemeier, 'The Theological Message of Hosea: Its Preaching Values', in *Review and Expositor*, Volume 72, No.4, 1975, pp 473-485. See also her *The Old*

Testament and the Proclamation of the Gospel, Westminster Press, Philadelphia 1973.

3 'The Theological Message of Hosea', p. 474.

4 Roy F Melugin, in *Worship in the Hebrew Bible*, edited Graham M Patrick, Sheffield Academic Press, Sheffield 1999.

5 Ibid p. 250.

6 As does Walter Brueggemann, *Cadences of Home: Preaching among Exiles*, Westminster John Knox Press, Louisville 1997.

Chapter 4

1 eg *Surviving the Sermon*, Cowley Publications, Cambridge 1992.

2 'Preaching', *Methodist Recorder*, 9.12.93.

Chapter 5

1 James L Crenshaw, *Trembling at the Threshold of a Biblical Text*, Eerdmans, Grand Rapids 1994, p. 12.

2 Ibid p.14.

3 Donald E Gowan, *Reclaiming the Old Testament for the Christian Pulpit*, T & T Clark, Edinburgh 1980, pp. 145-146.

Chapter 6

1 *The Salvation Army Handbook of Doctrine*, International Headquarters of the Salvation Army, London 1969, p. 126.

Chapter 7

1 Michael Prior, *The Bible and Colonialism*, Sheffield Academic Press, Sheffield 1997.

2 14.2.2000.

3 SPCK, London 1998.

4 Ibid, pp. 4,11.

5 eg R W L Moberly, *Genesis 12-50*, JSOT Press, Sheffield 1992, pp. 39-56.

Chapter 8

1 Methodist Publishing House, Peterborough 1983.

2 In *Heaven shall not Wait*, Wild Goose Publications, Glasgow 1987, pp. 32-33.

3 See, for example, Robert Davidson's *The Courage to Doubt*, SCM Press, London 1983.

4 H Wheeler Robinson, *The Cross in the Old Testament*, SCM Press, London 1955.